T0286792

Cambridge Elements ≡

Elements in Music and the City
edited by
Simon McVeigh
Goldsmiths, University of London
Laudan Nooshin
City, University of London

MUSIC FROM ALEPPO DURING THE SYRIAN WAR

Displacement and Memory in Hello Psychaleppo's Electro-Tarab

Clara Wenz
University of Würzburg

CAMBRIDGE
UNIVERSITY PRESS

CAMBRIDGE
UNIVERSITY PRESS

Shaftesbury Road, Cambridge CB2 8EA, United Kingdom

One Liberty Plaza, 20th Floor, New York, NY 10006, USA

477 Williamstown Road, Port Melbourne, VIC 3207, Australia

314–321, 3rd Floor, Plot 3, Splendor Forum, Jasola District Centre, New Delhi – 110025, India

103 Penang Road, #05–06/07, Visioncrest Commercial, Singapore 238467

Cambridge University Press is part of Cambridge University Press & Assessment, a department of the University of Cambridge.

We share the University's mission to contribute to society through the pursuit of education, learning and research at the highest international levels of excellence.

www.cambridge.org
Information on this title: www.cambridge.org/9781009073004

DOI: 10.1017/9781009071765

First published 2023

A catalogue record for this publication is available from the British Library.

ISBN 978-1-009-07300-4 Paperback
ISSN 2633-3880 (online)
ISSN 2633-3872 (print)

Music from Aleppo during the Syrian War

Displacement and Memory in Hello Psychaleppo's Electro-Tarab

Music and the City
DOI: 10.1017/9781009071765
First published online: June 2023

Clara Wenz
University of Würzburg
Author for correspondence: Clara Wenz, clara.wenz@uni-wuerzburg.de

Abstract: Aleppo is regarded as one of the historical centres of an urban Arab art music tradition known as '*tarab*'. During the war that followed Syria's 2011 political uprisings, vast parts of the city were destroyed. This Element explores how tarab lives on in new contexts. It does so through a focus on the work of Hello Psychaleppo, one of Aleppo's displaced musicians and the pioneer of 'electro-tarab', an eclectic style of urban electronic dance music that is conceived as a homage to Aleppo's musical legacy. Whether using local religious chants, Palestinian poetry or the image of a yellow man, electro-tarab includes an inventory of audio, visual and literary samples. These samples help conceptualise the role music has played during the Syrian war; they offer insights into Aleppo's musical and diasporic afterlife; and they illuminate some of the socio-aesthetic parameters that characterise contemporary Arab electronic music.

Keywords: Aleppo, music during the Syrian War, music and displacement, electro-tarab, Arab electronic music scenes

ISBNs: 9781009073004 (PB), 9781009071765 (OC)
ISSNs: 2633-3880 (online), 2633-3872 (print)

Contents

1 Introduction

'They say punk is dead, I say *tarab* is dead and I am trying to bring it back.' This is how the Syrian electronic musician Samer Saem Eldahr described his musical mission when I first met him in Beirut in November 2016, a time when his hometown Aleppo was caught up in the Syrian war.[1] The Arabic term '*tarab*' has no adequate equivalent in English. Roughly translatable as 'ecstasy', it is applied to different urban art music repertoires of the Middle East as well as to the feeling of enchantment that these repertoires are said to generate in its performers and listeners. Besides these more generic definitions, tarab has also, as we shall see, been mythologised as Aleppo's endemic musical tradition. It is especially within this context that Hello Psychaleppo's musical mission should be understood. Taking his statement about 'wanting to bring back *tarab*' as its point of departure, this Element explores how Aleppo's musical legacy has been re-activated in times of conflict and displacement.

Throughout the past several years, Samer Saem Eldahr, better known under his artistic name Hello Psychaleppo (and referred to in the following using both names interchangeably),[2] has become an influential actor within the growing alternative and transnational Arab electronic music scenes. With his so far four albums *GOOL L'AH* (2013), '*HA!*' (2014), '*TOYOUR*' (2017) and *JISMAL* (2021), he is regarded as the pioneer of 'electro-tarab'. Conceived as an homage to the musical legacy of his hometown of Aleppo, this eclectic and experimental musical style combines global electronic dance music styles such as dub, dubstep, drum & bass, trap and trip-hop with (digital) Arab musical aesthetics. The latter consist, for example, of computer-generated microtones, *taqasim* (instrumental improvisations) played on a midi keyboard and, most importantly,

---

[1] Personal conversation, 16 November 2016. In addition to one extensive interview, which I conducted with Hello Psychaleppo in Beirut, my analysis draws from several more informal conversations held with him as well as other displaced Syrian musicians, artists and music aficionados between 2016 and 2021, attendance of two of Hello Psychaleppo's concerts (in 2016 and 2019 respectively), digital media content, as well as our joint public conversation on 'Electro-Tarab and the Role of Sampling in Times of Displacement', presented on 10 November 2020 in the framework of the London Middle East and Central Asian Music Forum. Interviews were conducted in both Arabic and English. In times when Syrians find large parts of their social and musical lives operating online, a state that has been propelled further by the Covid crisis, Internet platforms such as SoundCloud and YouTube constituted additional and important sites of digital fieldwork.

　　A brief note on transliteration: I have adopted the system of the *International Journal of Middle Eastern Studies* (IJMES), but, for matters of technical simplicity, left out diacritical marks indicating long vowels and emphatic consonants (for example, 'tarab' is rendered as 'tarab'). At times, I derive from this standard in order to convey local variants and colloquial dialect. For the names of Arab authors and musicians I have adopted the most widely accepted transliteration in English.

[2] I use Hello Psychaleppo when writing about his artistic practice and Eldahr when referring to his personal background (e.g. childhood memoires).

samples from old recordings, ranging from songs by local Aleppian musicians to the pan-Arab hits of Egyptian star singers such as Um Kalthoum (ca. 1904–1975), Abd al-Halim Hafiz (1929–1977) and Asmahan (1912–1944). Trying to characterise this fusion of styles, international media outlets have described electro-tarab in ways that evoke popular music icons, night club imagery and, at times, the sensationalist undertones of mainstream war reportage: 'Massive Attack meets Abdel Halim Hafez',[3] 'Um Kalthoum on Acid',[4] 'Tripping on Tarab',[5] 'dubstep that makes you want to both shake your booty while reading an encyclopaedia on Syrian history'[6] and, in the headline of a 2013 VICE article, 'Music to Listen to While Your Country Burns'.[7]

Indeed, born in Aleppo in 1989 and a former student at the city's Faculty of Fine Arts, Eldahr's musical practice and career developed against the background of the Syrian war. The way his musical life has unfolded throughout the past decade reads like the now hauntingly familiar story of forced migration, resident permits, visa applications and rejections. Having left Aleppo in 2012, the year that marked the outbreak of fighting between armed oppositional groups and Syrian regime forces, he first went to Beirut, not foreseeing that what was originally intended to be a temporary stay – he was setting up an exhibition in Beirut and had left many of his recordings back home – would last almost three years. Then, in 2015, a year after new visa restrictions imposed on Syrians under Egyptian president Sissi forced him to cancel his participation in the prestigious D-Caf festival for alternative music in Cairo, Lebanese authorities rejected the renewal of his residency permit. Forced to leave Beirut but unable to return to his war-ravaged hometown, Eldahr was eventually able to migrate to the United States where, despite being in possession of a green card, he was soon exposed to new travel restrictions. Donald Trump's 2017 travel ban not only forced him to cancel a show in the newly opened Elbphilharmonie in Hamburg (he feared he would not be able to re-enter the country afterwards), but also made it impossible for his parents to join or even visit him in the United States.

As indicated by his artistic name Hello Psychaleppo, it was Eldahr's musical practice that offered him a way to stay connected to his hometown from a distance. As he wrote in 2015, the year he moved from Lebanon to the United States:

---

[3] www.shubbak.co.uk/shahba/.

[4] www.ozy.com/good-sht/music-thats-like-umm-kulthum-on-acid/62358/.

[5] www.beirut.com/l/28824.

[6] https://readopium.wordpress.com/2015/03/10/hello-psychallepo/. The authors of the platform in which this interview was published have deleted their website. As a result, the online link to the interview is no longer available.

[7] www.vice.com/en_us/article/vdpev3/psychaleppo-music-to-listen-to-while-your-country-burns.

If you listen to my music very closely, you will find Syria behind every musical sign ['alamah] containing the memory of the place, the time and the people. I gather inside a musical note [nutah] what I could not take with me in my travel bag. This music is my consolation on my journey into the unknown [al-majhul].[8]

Scholars have studied (urban) musical styles as a means through which displaced populations, refugees, migrants and diasporic communities across the world re-enact a relation to their homeland and maintain a sense of community and cultural identity (see Baily & Collyer 2006; Hirshberg 1990; Levi & Scheding 2010; Lidskog 2016; Rasmussen et al. 2019; Reyes 1999).[9] Within this context, many have focused on musical performance and/or rituals of collective music-making, often framing their analyses in the pertinent but familiar tropes of preservation and acculturation. This Element approaches the relation between music, memory and displacement from a different angle, through a focus on one of the most significant characteristics of Hello Psychaleppo's music (and of contemporary Arab urban electronic music in general): the practice of sampling. In outlining how, with his use of samples, Hello Psychaleppo not only recontextualises historic tarab recordings but also aims at composing a musical memory of his hometown from afar, this Element contributes to the growing body of studies on the musical practices of Syrian diasporic and refugee communities, which to my knowledge have so far exclusively focused on Syrians living in Istanbul (Habash 2021; Hajj 2016; Öğüt 2021; Shannon 2016, 2019).

1.1 Aleppo from Samples

From the rise of the sound collage techniques of *musique concrète* developed by Pierre Schaeffer and others in the 1940s, the revolutionised use of the sampler as the 'quintessential rap production tool' (Rose, 1994: 93) of black US hip-hop scenes in the 1980s, to the now widespread co-option of pre-recorded music by global music mass industries, throughout the past century, the practice of *sampling* (the [digital] copying of portions of a pre-existing sound recording to be re-used in another composition or song) has been an integral part of diverse musical traditions. In contrast to scholars who have studied sampling practices through the lens of ownership and copyright (McLeod & DiCola 2011) or viewed them as symptomatic of postmodern self-referentiality (Manuel 1995), a global age of digital reproduction (Goodwin 1988), or the seductions of neoliberal and consumer culture (Taylor 2016), my analysis follows scholars who have looked at sampling practices in a more localised context. Arguably one of the most important scholars to cite here is

---

[8] www.syrianeyesoftheworld.com/2015/01/23/samer-saem-eldahr/. Translated from the Arabic citation.
[9] The sources here only constitute a selection. For a recent overview of existing literature on the subject, see Stokes 2020.

Tricia Rose, author of the pioneering *Black Noise: Rap Music and Black Culture in Contemporary America* (1994). Rose argues against the mischaracterisation of sampling within US hip-hop cultures of the 1980s as simply a by-product of global digital and technological developments. Instead, she points out how early rap producers used sampling techniques in ways that affirmed, built on and re-shuffled existing musical, oral and poetic traditions of Afro-diasporic people while at the same time articulating their own social realities, worldviews and approaches to sound and community (Rose 1994: 104). Rose's call to understanding the sampling practices of early US rap scenes as a form of cultural and intertextual reference is directed at a US context, yet her insistence on the need to *historicise* sampling practices is of great importance to my argument.

Following her approach, this Element analyses the sampling practices of Hello Psychaleppo (as well as some of his contemporaries) in three different but interrelated ways: (1) as a way to narrate memories of Aleppo's musical history in times of war; (2) as a technique that allows for the emergence of new urban musical styles at times when access to local musical knowledge has been lost; and (3) as a form of musical 'coding' that can forge and sustain, if only temporarily, a sense of home and community in times of displacement. Focusing less on their sonic than their symbolic quality, I include in my analysis not only the digitally sourced sound extracts that Hello Psychaleppo integrates into his music, but also other visual, literary and tactile references that form part of his and other contemporary Syrian electronic musicians' artistic practices.

This Element is divided into three main sections. Section 2 provides an over-view of the Syrian war and its effects on Aleppo's musical life, outlining how the city's mythic legacy as one of the cradles of tarab music is perpetuated and revived inside and outside of Syria. This will provide the necessary background to return to the work of Hello Psychaleppo and outline how he roots electro-tarab in the musical worlds of his hometown. Beginning with a description of an audio-visual homage to Aleppo that Hello Psychaleppo published in 2015, Section 3 identifies electro-tarab as part of a transnational alternative Arab music scene. It demonstrates how for Hello Psychaleppo and many others, the practice of sampling is an aesthetic strategy which, conditioned by a history of migration and displacement, allows them to affiliate with a cultural heritage and different notions of 'tarab' in times in which access to local musical knowledge and practices has been lost. Presenting the reader with ethnographic snapshots of a concert in Beirut in November 2016 at a time when Aleppo was under siege, Section 4 traces the particular *afterlife* that the city takes in electro-tarab, by exploring the different historical connections that take shape around some of the samples used in this concert. Whether fragments of a non-metrical *madih*, a praise of the prophet Muhammad as it was once recited in an Aleppian mosque, a Palestinian poem, excerpts from a speech by the former Libyan president Ghaddafi or a song by the Egyptian superstar Um Kalthoum, I will outline how these samples pave a path of (nostalgic) return to the places and communities that Hello Psychaleppo and many other Syrians have left behind while also functioning as a commentary on the history of displacement that currently shapes the lives not only of Syrians but of many others in and from the region. I conclude by reflecting on how the culture of tarab, by integrating an experience of loss into musical pleasure and a shared sense of intimacy, lives on in new musical and social contexts.

1.2 Tarab in New Contexts

By situating Hello Psychaleppo's electro tarab both in the socio-historical context of the Syrian war and a contemporary history of musical hybridity and electronic experimentation in the Arab world, this Element adds a new angle to existing studies on tarab. Scholars have explored tarab as traditional Arab music's 'ecstatic feedback model' (Racy 1991); they have identified it as 'enchantment' provoked by the legendary Um Kalthoum (Danielson 1997); they have studied its roots in Sufi musical rituals (Frishkopf 2001); they have traced its correlation to the perception of cassette sermons of the Islamic Revival movement in Egypt (Hirschkind 2006: 32–66); and they have analysed its role in formulating collective claims to alternative concepts of modernity in post-colonial Syria (Shannon 2006), to name some of the most prominent English-language studies.

Despite these diverse and wide-ranging approaches, no scholarly publication has yet been dedicated to the role of tarab in contemporary (electronic) popular music cultures across the Middle East and its diasporas.[10] Indeed, focusing on pre-2000s musical practices, most studies of Arab music have adopted a rather narrow approach, whether by exclusively associating tarab with high-art, pre-First World War repertoires or by rationalising it as 'traditional' and opposed to Western music. As Racy states at the beginning of *Making Music in the Arab World,* which counts as the standard work on the subject: 'Totally extraneous to this domain [the tarab community] are Western and Arab performers and composers of European music' (2003: 15).[11]

In outlining the ways in which electro-tarab is at home both in an Aleppian musical culture and in the Arab world's transnational electronic

---

[10] For a noteworthy exception, see Fulton-Melanson 2021.

[11] The anthology *The Arab Avant-Garde: Music, Politics, Modernity* (Burkhalter et al. 2013) is an example of a piece of scholarship that attempts to challenge such perspectives. Tracing a history of musical hybridity and globally engaged innovation within the Arab world – from the Egyptian Nahda composer Sayyed Darwish, the Lebanese Rahbani family, to the Iraqi-born performer Aida Nadeem – the authors formulate a critique of the totalising perspective of the scholarship on 'traditional' Arab music that obscures other, more experimental musical practices in the region (for instance, Farmer 1930; Racy 2003; Touma 1996).

music scene, this Element proposes to shift the focus away from discussions of authenticity that characterise existing literature towards an investigation of the (political) spaces and imaginaries that are associated with this musical culture today. Hello Psychaleppo has a far smaller audience than many other actors in this scene, not to mention the many tarab artists that he samples. However, as I will discuss, his musical practice (as well as the artistic responses and fan reactions that it has provoked) have worked to create a language that helps conceptualise the role tarab music has come to play in the context of the Syrian war and illuminates some of the main socio-aesthetic parameters that characterise contemporary Syrian/Arab urban electronic music cultures.[12]

A powerful example that illustrates this is a piece of artwork (Figure 1) that the Syrian graphic designer Sedki al-Imam produced for the 2018 song 'Ya Wela', a collaboration between Hello Psychaleppo and the Jordanian-Palestinian vocalist and member of the band 47 Soul, El Far3i. The graphic shows a music control panel whose buttons are labelled as follows : '*Ḥalab* [Aleppo]' and '*ghazza* [Gaza]'; '*muqawamah* [resistance]'; '*tahjir* [displace-ment]' and '*al-ʿoudah* [return]', as well as 'Taha Hussein', the name of a twentieth-century Egyptian writer and intellectual who, as a key figure of the Arab/Ottoman period of cultural and political reform known as *nahda* ['renaissance/rebirth'], is being remembered as having promoted the selective adoption of Western culture, ideas and techniques with the aim of strengthen-ing the Arab world's own politics, religion, art and culture (Burkhalter et al. 2013: 15).

The connection drawn between Aleppo and Palestine, the evocation of shared histories of forced migration and resistance, the production of new, global, but culturally rooted Arab musical forms, and the wish to return to places that were left behind or destroyed during war: as the following pages will demonstrate, these themes are not only encoded in Hello Psychaleppo's electro-tarab, they also shape the practices, narratives and memories of many other (electronic) musicians and aficionados from the region.

2 '*Im al-Tarab*': Musical Myths and Afterlives

With over 300,000 civilians killed, 6.7 million internally displaced and more than 6.6 million refugees worldwide, the Syrian war has generated one of the

---

[12] Adopting this language as one of my analytical frameworks helps to establish this book's conditions of 'coevalness', a term which, coined in Johannes Fabian's *Time and the Other*, runs counter to what he refers to as the 'persistent and systematic tendency to place the referent(s) of anthropology in a Time other than the present of the producer of anthropological discourse' (Fabian 1983: 31, quoted in Behdad 1994: 6).

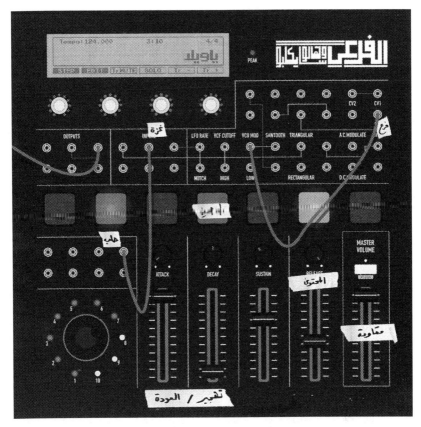

Figure 1 Cover art for 'Ya Wela' Courtesy of Sedki al-Imam

largest human catastrophes and histories of forced migration of this century.[13] Although the roots of the conflict reach back far into the past century (see Munif 2020: 96–119), its more immediate historical context has been the transnational movement of anti-government protests which, in late 2010, began to stretch from Tunisia across Egypt, Yemen, Bahrain and Libya, and which became known as the Arab Spring.

In Syria, the first larger-scale protests broke out in the southern town of Der'a in early March 2011, after security forces arrested and allegedly tortured fifteen schoolchildren who were accused of having graffitied '*al-sha'b yurid isqat al-nizam* [the people want the downfall of the regime]'

---

[13] These numbers are based on a 2021 UNHCR and a 2022 OHCHR report (though questioned by many and considered to be higher). The death toll does not include non-civilian and indirect deaths (i.e. those that resulted from a conflict-related lack of access to essential goods). Most externally displaced Syrians currently reside in neighbouring countries, above all Turkey, Lebanon and Jordan. Others have fled to Europe, especially Germany, or sought refuge elsewhere across the world.

onto the walls of a local school – a slogan which by then was being chanted by millions of protesters across the Arabic speaking world.[14] The outrage that the children's arrest and torture sparked among their family members and local citizens, who took to the streets to demand the children's release and the persecution of those responsible for their abuse, was met with brutal state violence and eventually led to country-wide solidarity protests. The towns of Der'a, Homs, Hama, Lattakia, Idlib, Deir az-Zor, as well as Damascus and later Aleppo – the country's two largest cities – saw hundreds, and sometimes thousands, of people take to the streets, and civil activists formed so-called Local Coordination Committees to organise a popular movement they hoped would end the autocratic rule of Bashar al-Assad and the military-Baathist dictatorship he had inherited from his father, Hafiz al-Assad, who had ruled Syria from 1971 until his death in 2000. Yet the repression of protests continued, and the regime's escalating use of violence against dissidents, activists and civilians eventually led to the formation of armed oppositional groups made up of military defectors and volunteers, most prominently the Free Syrian Army (FSA). Their violent confrontation with regime security forces, the gradual co-opting of the uprising by radical Islamic groups, as well as the growing involvement of foreign actors, especially Russia, eventually turned what had started out as a largely peaceful struggle for citizen rights and political transformation into a full-scale militarised war.

Aleppo, Syria's largest city, became a key centre of the regime's counter-insurgency campaign, when in the summer of 2012, armed oppositional fighters – many from Aleppo's poorer and more conservative rural hinterland (Yassin-Kassab & al-Shami 2016: 94–5) – gained control over East Aleppo. Now effectively divided into a regime-held West and an opposition-held East, Aleppo was drawn into a conflict that lasted more than four years, killed tens of thousands of its residents and drove hundreds of thousands out of their homes and, in many cases, out of their country and into exile. In late 2016, when the Syrian military's offensive on East Aleppo was entering its final phase, images that showed heavily bombarded neighbourhoods and the ordeal of those residing in areas under siege circulated widely across the world. Then, on 13 December 2016, a ceasefire marked the beginning of

---

[14] For an excellent analysis of the Arab Spring and its violent aftermaths, see Achcar 2013 and 2016. For works that specifically focus on the Syrian uprising and war, see, among others, al-Haj Saleh 2017; Ismail 2011; Munif 2020; Pearlman 2017; Wedeen 2019; and Yassin-Kassab & al-Shami 2016. For the role that art, including music, has played within the Syrian protest movement, see Halasa, Omareen & Mahfoud 2014; Lenssen 2020; Parker 2018; Silverstein 2012; as well as 'The Creative Memory of the Syrian Revolution', an online platform that archives Syrian revolutionary art: www.creativememory.org.

a (forced) 'population transfer' of more than 35,000 residents from East Aleppo to the western countryside and Idlib province, and Aleppo was officially retaken by the Syrian regime.[15]

2.1 Aleppo's Legacy: Tarab in Times of War

While the effects of the Syrian war on Aleppo's infrastructure and inhabitants have been devastating, it also left a profound impact on the city's cultural and musical life. Before the war, Aleppo had long been regarded one of the musical centres of the Middle East, as expressed in one of the city's famous nicknames. Besides *al-Shahba* ['the Grey/White One'], referring to the colour of the city's characteristic marble stone architecture, Aleppo is also known among residents as '*Im al-tarab* [the mother/cradle of tarab]'. As stated earlier, tarab, roughly translatable as 'ecstasy' in Arabic, is an aesthetic expression with a variety of meanings and uses. First, it denotes particular musical styles, repertoires and performance contexts. Once used to refer to art music traditions rooted in the Eastern Arab world *prior* to the First World War, the term is today applied more generically to urban art repertoires native to cities such as Aleppo, Damascus, Beirut, Jerusalem or Cairo. Second, tarab signifies musically induced moments of emotional uplifting, enchantment and rapture that are traditionally believed to be produced when performing and/or listening to these repertoires (see Racy 2003).

Aleppo's musical nickname operates on several geographical levels. First, it highlights the city as one of the region's historic centres of tarab music: particularly during the first half of the twentieth century, Aleppo was home to some of the Middle East's most famous tarab musicians and composers. Omar al-Batsh (1885–1950), Bakri al-Kourdi (1909–78), Ali al-Darwish (1872–1952), Muhammad Khairy (1935–81) and Sabah Fakhri (1933–2021) are renowned across the Arab world for their musicianship, especially for their mastery of repertoires typical to Aleppo. These include the pre-composed *muwashshaḥ* and the improvised *mawwal* – both poetic vocal forms sung in classical Arabic – as well as the *qudud ḥalabiyyah*, a genre of light popular songs usually performed in local dialect. Commonly integrated into a suite known as the *wasla*, these vocal genres are performed in both sacred and

---

[15] A detailed timeline of the conflict in Aleppo is provided by the Aleppo Project based at the Centre for Conflict, Negotiation and Recovery of the Central European University's School of Public Policy in Budapest (since 2019 and due to changes to the National Higher Education law under Hungary's prime minister Viktor Orbán, the university has relocated to Vienna). The Aleppo Project is a collaboration between Syrian refugees, Syrian and non-Syrian students, academics, policy experts and others aiming to preserve and collect material on Aleppo's cultural heritage as well as explore possible ways of rebuilding urban life after conflict: www.thealeppoproject.com/conflict-timeline/.

secular contexts (Poché 2001; Shannon 2003a).[16] Second, Aleppo's musical nickname gives insights into Syria's cultural identity on a national level. In *Among the Jasmine Trees: Music and Modernity in Contemporary Syria*, a pioneering (and currently the only) monograph-length English ethnography on music performed inside Syria, the anthropologist Jonathan Shannon (2006: 27) writes the following about Aleppo's musical status:

> Although some Syrians questioned my interest in Arab music and even the existence of 'Arab' music altogether, almost no one questioned my desire to study that music – of whatever origin it might be – in Aleppo. . . . Although Damascus, as a result of the traditional rivalry between the two ancient cities, might challenge Aleppo's claim to fame in architecture, literature and cuisine – to just name a few domains – few would challenge Aleppo's role as a great center for music. Indeed, Damascenes and others from elsewhere in Syria commonly assert their musical identity by praising Aleppo's achievements, especially in contrast to the more often recognized achievements of Egyptian musicians. Aside from recognizing the 'Big Three' of famous modern Arab musicians – the Egyptian artists Umm Kulthūm, Muḥammad ʿAbd al-Wahhāb, and ʿAbd al-Ḥalīm Ḥāfiẓ – many Syrians argue that 'true' Arab music is found in Syria, not Egypt.

Unsurprisingly, ask a proud music aficionado from Cairo and you are likely to receive a different history lesson. Yes, the response may be, Aleppo *was* an important centre of traditional Arab music, but its status as *the* cradle of music is an exaggeration, a myth believed to have been spread by the Aleppian composer, nay-player and music theorist Ali al-Darwish during his participating in the First International Congress of Arab Music in Cairo in 1932. There, he, alongside the French musicologist Baron d'Erlanger, presented a classification of Arab modes and rhythms that, as some would claim, were far from being 'objective' but heavily influenced by Aleppian musical practice (see Katz 2015: 122–3; Iino 2009).

Yet as the American anthropologist William Bascom (1965: 4) once asserted, it is one of the main characteristics of a myth that it is only necessary for it to be believed by the society in which it is told. Thus, on a third level, and as an expression that is predominantly self-descriptive, Aleppo's musical nickname gives insights into the cultural and social consciousness of its residents. As one of them once explained to me: 'Tarab is one of the pillars of life in Aleppo [*waḥid min arkan al-ḥayah*], you know, like the five pillars of Islam. We cannot live without it.' Indeed, whoever investigates the reasons for their city's musical

---

[16] For a collection of Aleppian *muwashshaḥat*, see the song book *Min kunuzina: al-Muwashshaḥat al-Andalusiyyah* [From Our Heritage: The Andalusian Muwashshaḥat] (Raja'i & Darwish 1955). A collection of transcriptions of Aleppian *qudud* can be found in Dalal 2006a.

reputation will prompt many Aleppians to proudly point out the city's geographical location on the former Silk Routes and its historic importance as a centre of commerce and a place, not only of economic, but also of religious, social and cultural crossings. Just like its food, many will say, Aleppo's musical repertoires reflect the city's ethnic and religious mix of Arabs, Armenians, Kurds, Assyrians, Muslims, Christians and, until recently, Jews.[17] And one may be encouraged to listen to local repertoires and *hear* in them the city's historic engagement between Ottoman and Arab culture and its exposure to the influence of Egypt, France or the nearby Syro-Iraqi desert (Poché 2001).

Another important reason for Aleppo's status as a cradle of music, one may learn, is its role as historic centre of religiosity and religious mysticism. One will frequently come across the assertion that in Aleppo, musical talent is a gift (*mawhibah*) from God which is 'born' and perpetuated among the religious classes. One may hear Aleppians proudly describe their mosques, churches and former synagogues as 'conservatories' of ancient (Arab, Jewish, Assyrian or pre-Islamic) music or read that some of the city's most famous musicians were members of one of the city's many Sufi orders, acted as muezzins at local mosques and/or were trained in Quranic recitation (Racy 2003: 25; Shannon 2006: 106–7). Others will relate that the city's most famous singer Sabah Fakhri (1933–2021) is recorded in the *Guinness Book of Records* for the longest concert ever held: a fourteen-hour performance given to the Syrian community in Venezuela. Finally, in the dustier corners of the library of the School of Oriental and African Studies (SOAS) in London, one may come across an old folktale that has a local judge express the esteem with which Aleppians regard good music: instead of punishing a young boy who, hiding in the branches of a tree, had urinated on four drunk stone cutters because their singing failed to musically enchant him, the judge rebuked him for not having defecated on them and justified his judgement with the following words: 'He who composes and sings without producing tarab, must hear and get what he does not like' (Tahhan 2008; Tahhan & Rugh 2005: 33–6).

Above all, then, Aleppo's alleged legacy as cradle of musical ecstasy fulfils the role that the cultural geographer Moaz Azaryahu (2007: 23) has defined as typical of a city's nickname and mythic reputation: it is an expression of 'civic pride'. And in this function, it was, from the very beginning of the Syrian uprising, implicated in the construction of competing concepts of the nation. In the early years of revolutionary activism, vocal leaders of anti-regime demonstrations in oppositional-held east Aleppo were commonly referred to as *mutrib*

---

[17] For studies on the musical and liturgical heritage of Aleppo's former Jewish communities, see Kligman 2009; Shelemay 1998; and Wenz (in press). For a study on the musical and religious practices of Aleppo's Syriac Christians, see Jarjour 2018.

al-thawrah ('*mutrib*' is the name used for a distinguished vocalist of tarab music; '*al-thawra*' means 'revolution'). Moreover, it was often through the already mentioned Aleppian *qudud*, a repertoire of local songs frequently sung during weddings and closely associated with the culture of tarab, that protesters gave voice to their experience and political demands. They did so by replacing original lyrics, which often revolve around themes of romantic longing, with words that depicted the daily struggles of life under siege. A striking example of this is the song '*al-bulbul nagha 'ala ghusn al-full* [the nightingale sang from the branch of the jasmine tree]', famously sung by the legendary Aleppian singer Sabah Fakhri. In an instance of tragic comedy, protesters in the besieged neighbourhood of Bustan al-Qasr changed its original lines from 'we were six at the spring, the loved one came, then we were seven [*kinna sitah 'ala al-nab'ah ija al-mahbub sirna sab'ah*]' to 'we were one hundred at the mosque, a barrel bomb came down and we were seven [*kinna mi'eh fi al-jam'a nizl barmil sirna sab'ah*]', causing crowds of protesters to temporarily laugh not only at the brutality of the regime's aerial bombardments but also at their social distance from the history of state patronage that such songs are often associated with.[18]

Conversely, in June 2017, about half a year after east Aleppo had been retaken by the Syrian regime, Aleppo's first 'post-war' concert was staged as a victory celebration at the city's old citadel and headlined by state media with the title 'After Years of Emaciation, Aleppo Has Returned as the Cradle of Musical Ecstasy [*b'ad sanawat 'ijaf halab 'adat im al-tarab*]'.[19] 'Aleppo, what did they do to you! They destroyed your past in madness [*Shahba wish 'amilu fiki bi-junun haddu madiki*]': this is the chorus of the song that hundreds of attendees were prompted to sing in unison, reminiscent of Roland Barthes' (2013 [1957]) observation that myths tend to act out the ideology and world views of the ruling class and enacting not so much a musical comeback but the remaking of national culture and the return of Aleppo to the Syrian state. It is probably in knowledge and anticipation of such political spectacles that the Syrian oppositional journalist Fouad Abd al-Azzis, in an article published on 31 October 2016, called upon his readers to suspend all musical enjoyments, arguing that Aleppo's musical legacy had historically served the regime to

---

[18] Of the many tarab musicians who have been associated with Syria's state-promoted high culture, Sabah Fakhri was arguably the most prominent, not least since he (unsuccessfully) ran for a seat in the Syrian parliament in 1994, with campaign posters presenting him as 'The Righteous Son of Aleppo' (Shannon 2006: 133). For a recording of Fakhri singing the original version of this song, see www.youtube.com/watch?v=zaZVDj88G2Y. A full translation of its original lyrics can be found in Shannon 2018: 158–9. For a recording of the song as it was adapted during protests in Bustan al-Qasr, see www.youtube.com/watch?v=L5Y_kE6XCx4&t=453s.

[19] www.cambridge.org/Wenz.

naturalise the city as the cultural capital of the Baathist state and cover up its history of oppositional activism.[20]

Contrary to such nationalist orchestrations of musical meaning, for many Syrian migrants and refugees, Aleppo's musical legacy has offered a way to sustain a sense of identity in the disorienting times of war. From Berlin[21] to Istanbul (Habash 2021; Shannon 2016, 2019), Aleppians (and Syrians more generally) have activated a memory of tarab to evoke their country's high art music traditions and relate, from a distance, to the cultural memory of their hometown. Indeed, in times in which global perception of Aleppo has been dominated by images of violence and destruction, the perpetuation of its musical reputation has given testimony to the belief that a city resonates and 'lives on' in the memories of its former residents and communities.

2.2 The *Sammiʿah*: Ideal Types of Musical Affection

A vivid example of the ways in which music can temporarily 'recover' such memories is provided in an article that the Lebanese online newspaper *al-Modon* published in the summer of 2016. In it, France-based Aleppian journalist Omar Kaddour describes the images that come to his mind when listening to old records of Aleppian songs today, images that make him recall the imprint and affect that music had on the city's residents. He tells of friends who would stay up until dawn to hear the call to prayer and be enchanted by the musical virtuosity of Aleppo's muezzins; of neighbours climbing onto their roofs to stand and listen to the mesmerizing tunes of a famous *qanun*-player; even the city's birds had an appreciation for music, writes Kaddour, as they would regularly assemble on the edge of a courtyard's water fountain to listen to the songs emanating from the city's old town. Summoning up Aleppo's mythic legacy as a 'place of music', he concludes: 'I left Aleppo already many years ago, but when I listen to her from time to time, I tell myself: All cities are seen. Only Aleppo is seen and *heard* [*kul al-mudun tura, waḥdaha ḥalab tusmaʿ wa tura*].'[22]

'The mythic city', writes Moaz Azaryahu (2007: 19), 'mediates between the city as a geographical actuality and the city as a cultural phenomenon. . . . the mythic city represents a culturally shared worldview: it both constitutes the city as a well-defined entity with a distinct personality and establishes a community that shares the mythic city as a common worldview'. Indeed, when stating that 'Aleppo is heard', Omar Kaddour not only attaches himself to his city, but also

---

[20] www.zamanalwsl.net/news/article/74637/.

[21] https://ze.tt/ekstase-auf-orientalisch-deutschland-feiert-tanzt-und-lacht-zu-syrischer-musik/.

[22] www.cambridge.org/Clara.

associates himself with a community, and more precisely a community of
listeners. Two years after his article's publication, I met him during a brief
stopover at the Gare d'Austerlitz in Paris and he explained this attachment to me
in the following words:

> It is a personal thing: Despite my separation from Aleppo and the fact that I left
> it years ago ... even after ten years, my ear stayed in this place [*dallet udhni fi
> had al-makan*]. The marks of the place [*athar al-makan*] stayed present with
> me. It is a form of belonging [*intima'*], a sentiment [*al-wujdan*] ... The idea is
> about the speciality of Aleppo, that the Aleppian listens [*al-ḥalabi byesm'a*], he
> listens in a good way [*byesm'a bi-shakl jayyed*].[23]

In Aleppo, the idea of 'good listening' has traditionally been embodied by the
so-called *sammi'ah*. The *sammi'ah* (from the Arabic root s-m-'a, 'to listen') are
expert and connoisseur listeners, who, besides the musicians, are regarded as
the main constituent of the '*ahl al-tarab* [the people of tarab]'. During a singer's
performance and when registering musically virtuosic and emotionally uplifting
moments, the sammi'ah will respond with exclamations such as '*Ah!*', '*Allah!*',
'*Ya 'ayni!* [Oh, my eye!]' or '*Ya ruḥi!* [O my soul]'. These ecstatic sighs of
musical affection are meant to encourage a singer/musician to enchant the
audience further, and by registering musically virtuosic and emotionally uplifting moments, they also serve as a pedagogical device for less musically
educated audience members. In other words, they act as sonic markers that
both testify to and actualise what Georgina Born (2013: 35) has defined as
a 'musical public', 'an aggregation of the affected, of those participating in or
attending to a musical or sonic event'.

    While the sammi'ah exist across Syria (see Shannon 2006), the entire Eastern
Arab world (see Danielson 1997 and Racy 2003) and elsewhere,[24] Aleppians
will claim that their sammi'ah are the best. Their legacy is celebrated in an
anecdote that belongs to one of Aleppo's most frequently told urban myths. The
story concerns the Egyptian star singer and composer Muhammad Abd al-
Wahhab (c. 1901–91) and his first visit to Aleppo, during which he was
scheduled to give two concerts. During the first one, so it is commonly related,
he stood, to his astonishment, before an audience that consisted of only
a handful of people – the sammi'ah. They, so tradition had it, would 'test'
a musician coming to perform in Aleppo to see if he or she was worthy of their
city's residents' ears. Despite his disappointment with the low turnout, Abd al-
Wahhab decided to perform anyway, a decision that he was wise to make.

---

[23] Personal conversation, 18 October 2018.
[24] For an account of a similar institution of connoisseur listeners in North Indian classical music
known as *Rasikas*, see Alaghband-Zadeh 2017.

During the second night, and after the sammi'ah had spread the news about his great musicianship, the concert hall is said to have overflowed with more than 2,000 people. It is this incident, Aleppians will proudly claim, that ultimately determined Abd al-Wahhab's fame (see Shannon 2006: 31–2).[25]

Yet Aleppo's sammi'ah are much more than cultivated musical experts and critics. In the Aleppian popular imagination, they are considered to be what Judith Becker (2004: 2) has described as 'deep listeners': 'persons who are profoundly moved, perhaps even to tears, by simply listening to a piece of music'. Stories circulate of them dying from being overwhelmed by the power of music (Shannon 2003c: 77) and Um Kalthoum is proudly reported to have rhapsodised about her Aleppian fans, who would come all the way to Cairo to attend her concerts: 'I would see their eyes whilst on stage, their hearts and ears were with me, they were the audience most affected by the rapture [*nashwa*] of voice, music and rhythm.'[26]

Aleppians' 'talent' for musical affection continues to be actively remembered from afar. In my conversations and encounters with former residents of the city, the sammi'ah often featured in their narratives as 'prototypes' of musical affection. Within this context, it was less their musical than their *emotional* expertise that was remembered. There was, for example, the sudden change of mimicry that my question about Aleppo's musical reputation provoked in the face of Yosef Antebi (1938–2021), a member of Syria's dismantled Jewish community, who emigrated from Aleppo to Tel Aviv in 1962. Enacting the reactions of an audience that he recounted as being 'drunk' from music, he imitated a crying face and shouted: 'They cry! They do "haah, hah!", "huuh", and "ahhh"!', to which he then added, with a lowered voice: 'Aleppians love a good mood [*al-ḥalabiyeen baḥebbu al-kayf*].'[27] In Berlin, Abu Farraj, the owner of the now torn-down Café Aleppo, stood up from his chair and shouted 'Allah!' to demonstrate that these 'ahhats' 'came from the heart [*heye tetl'a min al-qalb*]', that a real sammi'ah never 'simulated [*betsann'a*]' but 'rose up from his heart because he loved [*bequm min qalbu li'annu baheb*]'.[28] Later on, with his 'ud back on his lap and amidst the sweet-scented smoke and gurgling sounds

---

[25] According to Shannon, this incident is said to have happened in the 1930s. However, in a video clip of an interview in which Abd al-Wahhab tells this story himself, it is stated that it was 1924 when he first visited Aleppo. Wahhab relates how surprised he was when, during the first night, he found a group of elderly people sitting in front of him – some of whom he remembers smoking shisha – and how startled he was when during the second concert – he remembers it being held on a Saturday – more than 5,000 people are said to have attended. Asking one of the audience members to share the secret behind this strange occurrence, the answer he got was: '*Ḥalab balad al-dhawaqa* [Aleppo is the city of connoisseurs].' https://youtu.be/KwzQMC_4coQ.

[26] www.esyria.sy/ealeppo/index.php?p=stories&category=arts&filename=201007230905021.

[27] Personal conversation, 15 March 2017. [28] Personal conversation, 3 October 2016.

of his customers' shishas, Abu Farraj cited a verse that is commonly attributed to the eighth-century poet Bashar Ibn Burd. 'Sometimes, the ear loves before the eye [*al-udhnu ta'ashaqu qabla al-'ayni ahyanan*],' he stated, before relating how his own love for music was cultivated when, as a teenager strolling around Aleppo's old town, he entered the household shop of the famous Sheikh Sabri Moudallal (1918–2006), one of Aleppo's well-known religious chanters and the former muezzin of Aleppo's great Umayyad Mosque.[29] With his trademark sign of the Tarboush – the red-coloured, cylindrically shaped headdress worn by men during Ottoman times – Moudallal is viewed by many Aleppians as an embodiment of local authenticity and remembered dearly for his modest lifestyle, musical expertise and charming smile. And he is the subject of many anecdotes and stories that render him, in a way, a 'patron' of the sammi'ah. For instance, Lamis Sirees, an Aleppian-German vocalist based in Berlin, proudly recounts the approving stroke on the head that Moudallal once gave her as a child after she had presented her (evidently successful) rendition of a popular local song. Jonathan Shannon (2006: 192) vividly remembers how his sound recorder's mysterious failure to record the beauty of Moudallal's voice taught him to listen to the music he studied more carefully and, as he wrote, 'strive to remember [it] "on the back of the heart"'. And when young Abu Farraj entered Moudallal's shop to ask him for a cassette of 'Ḥilmi [My Dream]', one of Um Kalthoum's more difficult and sophisticated songs, Moudallal, so Farraj recounted, praised the young boy's 'accomplished ears' and thereby officially inaugurated his future life as a 'good listener [*sammi'a*]'.

As neatly captured in these comments, anecdotes and body gestures, the memory of Aleppo's famous connoisseur listeners cultivates not only a belief in the *effect* of music, it also rests on a recognition of the city's master musicians. Similar to what Jonathan Glasser has pointed out with regard to Andalusian repertoires in urban North Africa, in Aleppo the idea that the city acts as 'container' of a particular musical heritage is not only connected to particular localities but intimately linked to the concept of musical personhood and genealogy. Rather than simply being vested in the place itself, a local musical tradition is often thought to *reside* in and be transmitted by the people who come from that place and who are perceived as 'embodiments of the commitment to the local tradition' (Glasser 2016: 40).

---

[29] For a video clip (taken in 1993 by US ethnomusicologist Anne Rasmussen) showing Sabri Moudallal reciting the call to prayer from the Umayyad Mosque, see https://youtu.be/0IkHxe0rJyM. For more on Moudallal's biography and musical life, see Shannon 2006: 188–91 and Dalal 2006b [in Arabic], as well as the 1997 documentary '*Halab Maqamat al-Masarra* [Aleppo – Maqamat of Pleasure]', by Syrian filmmaker Mohammed Malas. A version with French subtitles can be found here: https://youtu.be/nPxoP3jgJSI.

Figure 2 Cover art for *Gool L'Ah* with an animation of the Egyptian singer Um Kalthoum Courtesy of Hello Psychaleppo

2.3 Electro-Tarab: A First Genealogy

This musical 'belief system', made up of Aleppo's mythical legacy as the cradle of tarab music [*Im al-tarab*], the ideal of the city's good listeners [*sammi'ah*], a commitment to local musical genealogies as well as the desire to experience moments of musical rapture [*tarab*] also motivates the work of Hello Psychaleppo (Samer Saem Eldahr). 'Tarab is a feel to music,' he explained during our conversation and, after taking a long pause to think, added, 'It's a very complex thing to explain. For example, when Abd al-Wahhab was asked "what is tarab?", he said, "when you say 'Allah'. This is it. That's how it affects you."'[30] It is precisely with this definition of tarab in mind that Hello Psychaleppo named his first album *Gool L'Ah* ('Say "Ah"' in Arabic – see Figure 2). With this title, he invites his audience to pay tribute to the legacy of Aleppo's famous connoisseur listeners and roots his practice in his hometown's traditional musical environments.

In a similar vein, when asked why his musical productions focus on tarab, he referred to his upbringing in Aleppo:

---

[30] Personal conversation, 16 November 2016. This definition of tarab has been reiterated numerous times; see Shannon 2006: 161.

> Tarab occupies a big part of me. I was raised in Aleppo, I would go sit in the cafes and what do they play? … They play Oum Kulthoum, Fairouz, Abd al-Halim, Nazem al-Ghazali. You get in a taxi, in the morning they play Fairouz, in the evening, Oum Kulthoum. This was the music that was the companion to my daily life. … I draw from tarab because that's where I'm coming from … We have a grammar and linguistic that's totally unique. I'm coming from this place, and I know its vocabulary.[31]

As already suggested in this comment, it is not a particular genre of tarab music that Hello Psychaleppo attempts to revive. Although he samples genres and musicians that are considered 'typically Aleppian' (examples will be discussed further in Sections 3 and 4.1), the music and sounds that he associates with his city also include the hits of Egyptian star singers Um Kalthoum, Abd al-Halim Hafiz and Asmahan, three pan-Arab cultural icons whose transregional fame was facilitated by a once thriving Egyptian film and record industry (which gained Cairo a reputation as the 'Hollywood of the Nile'). While these singers are associated with the urban tarab tradition and modern history of Egypt, mass-mediated as they are, they also have a history of mobilising local, national and pan-Arab identities across the region (see Danielson 1997; Lohman 2010; Stokes 2009). It is in this vein that Hello Psychaleppo re-inserts their music into a distinctively Aleppian urban imagery.

That Eldahr attributes his musical practice not only to his exposure to Aleppo's pan-Arab and mass-mediated sonic environment but to more local musical trajectories is also expressed in an anecdote that concerns his childhood encounter with legendary tarab singer Sabah Fakhri. According to Eldahr, it was Fakhri who predicted his musical career. Upon visiting Fakhri's house in Damascus with his father in the early 1990s when he was about two years old, Eldahr is said to have danced to a live recording of one of the singer's songs (Figure 3). Fakhri, so the story goes, immediately took notice of his musical talent and urged his father to take good care of his son, because he was 'going with the beat', a sign that he was 'going to have a career in music'.

Having one of the most important musical personalities of twentieth-century Aleppo and a prototype of Middle Eastern musical authenticity detect his musical talent links Eldahr to a lineage of musicians and religious chanters (*munshideen*) that can be traced back 200 years. Besides Fakhri, this chain of transmission includes his teacher, the famous composer and musician Umar al-Batsh (1885–1950), Ahmad Aqil (1813–1903) and al-Hajj Mustafa ibn al-Shaykh Abu Bakr al-Hariri al-Rifaʿi (1765–1855), also known as Bashank. As ethnomusicologist Lisa Iino (2009: 266) has documented, this chain of

[31] http://blog.mideastunes.com/post/145820971114/interview-with-hello-psychaleppo-on-turning.

Figure 3 Photograph showing young Eldahr dancing with the Aleppian
tarab legend Sabah Fakhri at his house in Damascus in 1992
Courtesy of Samer Saem Eldahr.

transmission leads straight into the religious heart of Aleppo's old town, and
more precisely into the Zawiyah Hilaliyah, one of the centres of these musicians' musical and educational activities.[32] One of Aleppo's many Sufi lodges,
the Zawiyah Hilaliyah belongs to the Qadiriyyah order and is located in
Aleppo's historic Jaloum quarter, which throughout the war was heavily
targeted by regime airstrikes.

Eldahr's narration of his encounter with Sabah Fakhri evokes a commitment to
the religious and musical world of Aleppo's old town, but how can such
a commitment be maintained in times when much of this environment has been
destroyed and most members of Aleppo's older generation of musicians are no
longer alive (two of the last representatives of this generation, Sabah Fakhri and
the religious chanter Hassan Haffar, died in 2021 and 2020 respectively)? Or, as
Jonathan Shannon (2019: 2172) asked in his article 'From Silence into Song:
Affective Horizons and Nostalgic Dwelling among Syrian Musicians in Istanbul':
'Because tarab and other affective terms in the urban musical lexicon of Syria can

---

[32] Literally 'corner' in Arabic, the term *zawiyah* denotes either a small mosque or prayer room, or
the part of a mosque dedicated to *dhikr* ceremonies and the performance of religious chants. For
an ethnographic account of a dhikr ritual held by Aleppo's Qadiriyyah order, see Shannon 2006:
106–29. For a discussion of the ritualistic aspects of Sufism in Syria and their relationship to the
country's official public sphere, see Pinto 2006 and 2016.

be understood as vehicles for the reproduction of social relationships of intimacy (Shannon 2006), what happens when these social relations are rent, and the music reverberates in new settings? Can there be homes for tarab and new Syrian tarab cultures outside of Syria?'

The following section attempts an initial answer to this question by offering the reader a perspective that contextualises Hello Psychaleppo's musical practice with contemporary sampling practices in and from the Arab world. The themes that arise from this perspective – hybridity, a revivalist impulse and the transnational connections and migratory paths of an Arab electronic and alternative music scene – will provide the background for understanding how the use of samples allows Hello Psychaleppo and many other contemporary Syrian electronic musicians to carry their own, personal notions of (Aleppian) tarab into new musical 'homes'.

3 *'Shahba'*: An Aesthetic of Displacement

The first scene of the video clip is opened by a crackling noise which sounds like blurred, faraway gunfire. The following three distorted piano chords and a slow trip-hop beat create a sonic texture that accentuates the shaky aesthetics of the slow-frame, minimalist animations that we, the viewers, are looking at. Everything is black and grey. Steam billows emanate from a tea glass that contains a vague, bubbly substance. Zooming into the glass from above, we hear scraps of a distant voice sounding out a gloomy, metallic 'aah'. Suddenly, we plunge. As we dive into the liquid, a heavy-hitting, drone-like bass sets in. Eventually, we surface on the other side and look straight into the blank face of a young man wearing glasses and long hair. He turns his head to stare through an open window which is framed by curtains that blow in the wind. All we can see is rain. First, through his eyes, then inside them, as a reflection of the outside world. Now the mumbling, distorted voice in the distance articulates the first clear word: 'Shahba!', it cries, 'Grey/White One!', calling Aleppo by one of its famous nicknames. Then it retreats, drowned out by the permeating bassline and the piano chords that are playing in a loop. We now see that the man sits on an armchair, with the cup of tea placed next to him on a table. He picks up a remote control and on a grainy, flickering TV screen appears real life footage of the old town of Aleppo. For a few seconds, we are taken through the city's historical market and past a stall that sells women garments. Back in his armchair, the young man watches and waits, first restless, then exhausted and bored, then, finally, with his eyes closed. As he opens them and stares back at the screen, we see the minaret of Aleppo's famous Umayyad Mosque and the pleading 'Shahba!' resonates for the second time. Haunted by a buzzing and accelerating beat, he picks up his cup of tea and drinks it in one, long gulp. The scene is penetrated by the distorted voice which now wails in a broken staccato: '*Li 'ajlek ana ghanet! Li 'ajlek ana ghanet!* [For you I sang! For you I sang']! Once he has swallowed the last drop of tea, the music takes off in rapid beats and arpeggios. On the TV appears a group of young boys who cheer into the camera, then Aleppo's old citadel comes into sight. The young man opens his eyes again and, coming to realise the effects of the magic substance that the cup of tea contained, gapes at his own metamorphosis: his hands recede into claws, his glasses, hair and mouth disappear; his nose turns into a beak. Now the bassline is softened by the sound of strings and he, transformed into a dove, peacefully flies over yesteryear's Aleppo as it looked like before the war. While the music fades out, we catch a last glimpse of the dove as it ascends from the chair into the sky. The window is left open, with the curtains blowing in the wind. Then, right after the closing credits and flashing up for no longer than a second, appears the animated drawing of a yellow man.[33]

Nowhere does Eldahr evoke his personal experience of displacement and his longing to return to Aleppo as explicitly as in the two-minute audio-visual homage to Aleppo, 'Shahba', that he produced in 2015 (Figure 4). Instead of only depicting his own, subjective memory of the city, he aimed at producing what he has called 'a composition of our collective memory'.[34] The images of Aleppo that flash up on the TV screen showing a city not yet destroyed by war were sourced from videos sent to him by friends; and the voice wailing in the background is that of the popular Aleppian singer Nihad Najjar (b. ca.1964). It is sampled from one of his most famous songs '*Aheen ya ḥalab* [Ah, O Aleppo]', which, released in the 1990s and composed to lyrics of the Aleppian poet Sufouh al-Shaghala (b. ca. 1956), is itself an homage to the beauty and heritage of Aleppo and as such well-known among its inhabitants. Finally, the animation of the yellow man that marks the end of the video depicts Abu Zakkour, one of Aleppo's better known residents who plays a prominent (and colourful) part in the city's popular memory. For the past thirty years or so, Zakkour has been exclusively wearing yellow and could usually be found hanging out in different places around town, to the notice of every passer-by, including once myself. Besides being the most colourful marker of collective Aleppian memory, Abu Zakkour has been the subject of various rumours and stories. Some think of him as the city's 'lucky charm' while others believe him to be secretly working as a spy for the *mukhabarat* (The Syrian secret service). During the war he was reportedly abducted by the Free Syrian Army but has recently re-appeared on the streets of Aleppo, explaining that he will continue to exclusively dress in yellow for as long as he lives.[35]

'Shahba' also engages with notions of memory and collective longing on a more symbolic level. Within the real-life footage of Aleppo's landmarks that the video includes, animated coloured ribbons wiggle their way through the otherwise gloomy scenery of Eldahr's hometown. Like 'threads of the mind', they preserve

---

[33] www.youtube.com/watch?v=MJDJ_o7Xlkc.

[34] https://www.shubbak.co.uk/a-collaborative-home-video-for-shahba-an-interview-with-hello-psychaleppo/.

[35] https://www.shubbak.co.uk/a-collaborative-home-video-for-shahba-an-interview-with-hello-psychaleppo/.

Figure 4 Cover art for 'Shahba' Courtesy of Samer Saem Eldahr

the memory of a city that no longer materially exists: they wind over women's dresses sold in the souq, Aleppo's centuries-old market, large parts of which were burnt down after fighting erupted in 2012; they move through the minaret of the Umayyad mosque which collapsed in 2013 after the surrounding area became one of the frontlines of the war; they whirl around a crowd of children who cheer into the camera and whose fate remains unknown to the viewer; and they slide down the walls of Aleppo's famous citadel, which, once a site of touristic leisure, became a garrison for regime snipers. At the end, the ribbons escape through the open window. These ribbons, the distorted voice of Nihad Najjar and the images – of Aleppo's landmarks, of Eldahr confined to watch his city on an armchair from afar, of his final transformation into a bird, as well as the animation of the yellow man that flashes up at the end of the video, a key to understanding his musical practice as we shall see in Section 4 – work to produce an aesthetic statement that has resonated among dispersed Syrian communities. As one YouTube commenter stated, 'it really describes how most Syrians are longing to go back to Shahba'.[36]

Eldahr himself stated a couple of months prior to the video's release: 'Through the visuals, I am trying to tell the viewer more about the music'.[37]

---

[36] www.youtube.com/watch?v=MJDJ_o7Xlkc.
[37] The Canadian online magazine *Reorient* in which this interview was published folded in 2018. As a result, the online link to the interview is no longer available.

It was only after hearing this description that I realised that the visual language of the 'Shahba' video not only spoke of a Syrian experience of displacement but could also be used as a metaphor to describe some of the motives, themes and impulses of the contemporary Arab electronic music scene that electro-tarab is part of. As will become clear in the following pages, not only can the colourful, animated ribbons that revolve around the black and white scenery of Aleppo's landmarks be seen as symbolising the ways in which many members of this scene conceive their musical practice as an homage to and *re-enchantment* of their home country's musical traditions; the ribbons' final escape through the open window may also be interpreted as illustrating how, in their musical practice, the presence of past sounds and voices is only fleeting and ultimately meant to pave the way for new (electronic) forms of music. Finally, the image of Eldahr confined to watch, listen to and remember his hometown from behind his TV not only tells of his longing to return, it also exemplifies a mode of media/music consumption that, shared by many of his Syrian contemporaries, has led to new forms of musical sociability.

3.1 Electronic Revivals: Transnational Arab Music Scenes

The international pop music industry has a history of utilising Arab musical records: for instance, Madonna's 1992 album 'Erotica' features a sample from the song '*Ana al-Um al-Ḥazina* [I am the sad mother]' that originally featured on the famous Lebanese singer Fairouz's 1962 album 'Good Friday: Eastern Sacred Songs'; Jay Z's 2000 hit 'Big Pimpin' is framed around a sample from the Egyptian superstar Abd al-Halim Hafiz's 1957 film song '*Khosara* [What a Pity]'; and the instrumental introduction to 'More Than A Woman' (2001) by R&B legend Aaliyah is taken from the song '*Aluli Ansa* [They told me to forget]' released in 1995 by the Syrian singer Mayada El Hennawy (see Frishkopf 2021). In the 2010s and 20s, European DJs, record collectors and re-issue labels such as Berlin's Habibi Funk or the French duo Acid Arab, to only name two prominent examples, are profiting from 'introducing' music from the Middle East and North Africa to urban nightclub scenes. An array of online platforms offer royalty-free samples of Arab vocals and percussion loops for music producers around the world and with the influx of Syrian migrants and refugees, European capitals have seen a proliferation of Arab party series and club nights such as Berlin's 'Arab Beats', the brainchild of Robert Soko, the creator of the city's famous 'Balkan Beats' nights from the 1990s. In short, Arab music has not only (covertly) informed the works of world-famous popstars, it has also turned into a promising marketing label for urban club culture industries.

Yet while the appropriation and commercialisation of Arab music by Western popstars, DJs and record labels has often been negatively associated with exoticism and generated debates about copyright and ownership from a post-colonial point of view[38] (in 2018, Jay Z won the copyright infringement lawsuit filed against him by one of Abd al-Halim Hafiz's relatives), it is important to note that the fusion of Arab musical styles with electronic musical cultures first and foremost has its roots in an ongoing history of musical hybridity *within* the Arab world. As scholars have pointed out, this hybridity is not the result of a singular historical process but is tied to different and often inter-related histories, including the rise of mass-media and technology (Armbrust 2001; Frishkopf 2010), histories of migration (Rasmussen 1996) and the experimental traditions of an Arab musical avantgarde (Burkhalter 2013; Burkhalter et al. 2013).

Electro-tarab is in many ways an example of such musical hybridity. Besides the heritage songs of traditional tarab musicians such as the already mentioned Sabah Fakhri, as well as the music of Led Zeppelin, Aphex Twin, Massive Attack, Infected Mushroom and Leonard Cohen, Hello Psychaleppo has cited his musical practice as being influenced by a more experimental Arab musical tradition. For example, he listens to the psychedelic fusions of Moroccan musician Abdou al-Omari from the 1970s and, in his use of the Moog synthesiser, has found inspiration in the works of Egyptian keyboardist Magdi al-Husseini, a former member of the ensemble of Abd al-Halim Hafiz. Moreover, his musical career, together with the recent proliferation of Arab EDM on dancefloors across the world, has been propelled by (and often developed in tandem with) the emergence of a 'New Wave', transnational and steadily growing Arab alternative music scene. Connecting Middle Eastern cities such as Cairo, Beirut and Ramallah to old and new urban centres of the Arab diaspora in Europe, Turkey and (to a lesser extent) the United States[39], this scene is made up of musicians, rappers, visual artists, graphic designers, cultural actors and fans and is sustained by a variety of independent platforms, festivals, initiatives, record labels, venues, radio stations and music magazines (Arab* Underground, Ma3azef, MARSM, Nawa Recordings, Raqs Amsterdam, Radio al-Hara, the recently closed Radio Beirut, Scene Noise, Shouka and Souq Records are only some of the names to be mentioned here).

---

[38] Such debates are also leaving a mark on the production of music technology. See, for example, the recent article 'Decolonizing Electronic Music Starts with its Software' regarding the release of free electronic music production software by British/Iraqi/Syrian musician and researcher Khyam Allami at Berlin's 2021 CTM festival for experimental art. Unlike Abelton and other software, that developed by Allami includes a tuning system that adapts to the microtonality of musical traditions such as those of the Arab world: www.pitchfork.com/thepitch/decolonizing-electronic-music-starts-with-its-software/.

[39] For an exploration of Arab EDM and 'post-tarab' scenes in Canada, see Fulton-Melanson 2022.

Rooted in the kind of DIY culture familiar from independent music scenes around the word, the musical styles associated with this scene range from experimental sound montages, acoustic singer-songwriter productions and rap to various Arab EDM styles such as 'Arab Deep House', 'Arab Techno', 'Arab Trap' and perhaps most prominently 'Electro-Dabke' by the popular UK-based Palestinian band 47 Soul. The latter is a combination of rural and synthesised Arab dance music known as dabke with global electronic music styles and lyrics that draw attention to the ongoing Palestinian struggle (Karkabi 2018). As diverse as these styles are, they have several things in common: (1) they are predominantly (though not exclusively) produced and consumed by members of a young and educated urban middle class; (2) they challenge what Boaventura de Sousa Santos (2018: 5) has called 'the dualistic, binary structure of Western imagination', an imagination which, in the realm of music, has tended to rationalise Arab music as 'traditional' and in opposition to 'modern' and 'Western' musical styles; (3) they tend to move through cultural spaces that, inflected by an active memory of the region's colonial history and its recent political uprisings, produce, consume and commodify alternative and/or electronic Arab music as musical 'underground'[40]; and (4) they are characterised by a revivalist and at times nostalgic impulse.

This impulse can, for a start, be observed in the choice of artists' names: The UK/Bahraini label 'Dar Disku' [House of Disco] is named after an Egyptian pop culture magazine from the 1970s; the band '47 Soul' evokes a Palestinian 'soul' prior to the establishment of the modern state of Israel in 1948, a name which, as anthropologist Nadeem Karkabi (2018: 187) argues, activates the memory of a pre-colonial geography not yet defined by the imposed and today often impassable borders of modern nation states; and members of Beirut and Amman's thriving hip-hop scene have anchored their rap in local poetic vocal traditions such as the *'ataba* or the *zajal* (Wiedemann 2019), incorporated samples of folk songs and instruments and given themselves artistic names that pay homage to musical ancestors from the region. Syrian born rapper *al-Darwish* (formerly Sayyed Darwish) evokes the memory of Sayyed Darwish (1892–1923), an Egyptian singer, composer and revivalist who is regarded as an early twentieth-century pioneer of Egyptian popular music; the Lebanese collective Fareeq el Atrash pays tribute to Farid al-Atrash (1910–74), a Druze Syrian singer and oud-player (and the brother of Asmahan) who, spending most of his career in Egypt, became one of the most popular musicians of his time; and the name of the Syrian rapper Bu Kolthoum is said to take its inspiration

---

[40] See Demerdash 2012 and Hawas 2012 for early explorations of the ways that 'revolutionary' Arab culture has been consumed and translated on a global stage.

from the Egyptian star-singer Um Kalthoum and the pre-Islamic Arab poet Ibn Amr ibn Kulthum.

Conceived as a *re-enchantment* of tarab, a tradition that as I have outlined has been mythologised as Aleppo's endemic music, Hello Psychaleppo's electro-tarab is in many ways an expression of a similar impulse of revivalism. Within this context, the use of samples only serves as an intermediary aesthetic strategy, for a vision of a form of music which goes far beyond the fusion of electronic beats with Arab music samples, as he explains:

> For me, having this 'electro-tarab-kind-of-thing' and focusing on sampling is not because this is the final art form. Electro-tarab can be a lot more than that in the future, I would say. For now, it is about sampling because we lack the talent . . . . I mean, back in the day, the number of singers . . . now we have one percent of what we had before, right? We had a lot of good composers, the forms were crazy, very different quality, right? So now, we lack this, and to have the sampling kind of thing, to understand the form, understand the writing, understand everything – that's a kind of bridge of what we had before and what's coming next. That can bring talent back . . . You can have people going back to writing, and I can tell, I mean people now are going for sampling, they really like the hype. Sometimes they lack some technical and music theory background but at least people feel the motivation to do something, they are proud of what they have. It's going to take another forty years, I would say, to have something that's coming back and to understand it from a new kind of perspective. . . . And it's not just me, there are a lot of people who put in a lot of effort to bring this kind of thing back. And with all the youngsters who have access to technology and computers, so to bring this back is going to be huge. Like Hip Hop. Everyone is doing like beats and stuff. It's happening.[41]

Indeed, the ways in which Arab electronic musicians and rappers mobilise the musical, cultural and political legacies of past musicians and geographies to inform their own musical practice appears to be characterised by the same kind of 'narrative originality' that Tricia Rose (borrowing a concept from American history and oral culture scholar Walter Ong (1982)) once attributed to members of the US rap scenes in the 1980s. Describing how members of these scenes used samples to produce music that paid homage to and drew from Black cultural traditions and musical styles, she writes:

> Sampling, as employed by rap producers, is a musical time machine, a machine that keeps time for the body in motion and a machine that recalls other times, a technological process whereby old sounds and resonances can be embedded and recontextualized in the present. Rap technicians employ digital technology as instruments, revising black musical styles and priorities

---

[41] Personal conversation, 16 November 2016.

through the manipulation of technology. In this process of techno-black cultural syncretism, technological instruments and black cultural priorities are revised and expanded. In a simultaneous exchange, rap music has made its mark on advanced technology, and technology has profoundly changed the sound of black music. (Rose 1994: 116)

Rose's account of the ways in which samples have allowed US rap producers to recall, revise and expand existing black musical styles helps understand some of the motivations, impulses and techniques that currently shape transnational urban Arab electronic music scenes. Further, her suggestion to think of sampling as a 'musical time machine' also lends itself to illuminate the more immediate historical context within which electro-tarab unfolds.

3.2 Virtual Networks: Sampling in a Syrian Context

Hello Psychaleppo's musical practice and his desire to revive tarab mark a moment of severe political crisis, cultural upheaval and a time in which displaced Syrians across the world have found themselves disconnected from the musical environments of their former homes. Enabled by the growing digitisation of Arab music and the fact that many songs that were previously disseminated in the form of vinyl, tapes, CDs or mp3 collections are now available on online platforms such as YouTube, the practice of sampling has become one way for musicians to stay connected. It is, in other words, an artistic strategy that is at least partly conditioned by a history of displacement. Not only does it allow Syrians to affiliate with a cultural heritage from afar and in times in which for many performers and audiences, access to local musical knowledge and face-to-face modes of musical contact has been lost; as Eldahr explained to me, one of the main reasons he uses samples is his desire to document and *archive* a musical and poetic heritage for a generation of Syrians born outside the country who, unable to return in the near future, are likely to grow up unfamiliar with the culture of their parents' homeland.

As such, Hello Psychaleppo is by far not the only displaced Syrian musician who samples the sounds and voices of his contemporaries and/or of musicians of the past. In Stockholm, Obay AlSharani has created ambient and trip hop tracks based on excerpts from historical records, including Farid al-Atrash's song '*Ya aḥla shi fi al-kawn* [O Most Beautiful Thing in the Universe]'; in Istanbul, OM. EL Beat, known for her satirical music videos such as 'I Love death' and 'ISIS Funk', has integrated samples of the Syrian 'World-Techno-Dabke' star Omar Suleiman who, ever since being discovered by the Sublime Frequencies Label in the 1990s, has collaborated with Björk and British producer and electronic musician Four Tet (see Silverstein 2016); in Beirut, Khaled

Allaf has fused the sounds of the *buzuq* and vocal poetic folk traditions of Syria and Lebanon's mountain region with Pink Floyd or Michael Franti and Spearhead's 'Ganja Babe'; in Vienna, Refugee A has set deep house rhythms to religious chants from Aleppo; the Hamburg-based band Shkoon, made up primarily of a German DJ and a Syrian vocalist from the town Deir az-Zoor, has toured across Europe and the Middle East presenting their audiences with live acts that 'merge oriental melodies with western electronic beats'[42]; while Colonel Abu Diab, based in Berlin, had his audience at the 2019 Fusion Festival dance to a set of SoundCloud-sourced 'bedroom productions', including a track originally released by the already mentioned UK-based Bahraini collective Dar Disku, which samples the famous song '*bas ism'a mini* [Just Hear from Me]' by Saria al-Sawas, a popular wedding singer from Syria's Homs governorate.

While these musical productions are contemporaneous with a wider sampling and global remix culture,[43] they also and often directly refer to Syria's contemporary history and evoke memories of specific localities. For example, quite a few Syrian electronic musicians have organised their music productions around memories of places they can no longer return to. The cover image of 'Moniety' (Figure 5), a track released by Berlin-based Syrian trio Nakriz in 2021, shows a man with Bedouin headgear and a background of ancient ruins. Following a digitally manipulated road sign, the man walks towards the East Syrian town of Raqqa. Located on the banks of the Euphrates River, Raqqa is not only the place of origin of the folksong that the track reproduces through vocals, down-tempo beats and the synthesised sounds of the *mijwiz* (a double-reed pipe) that is associated with many folk music traditions in the region; having served first as a stronghold of the opposition and then, between 2014 and 2017, as the proclaimed capital of the Islamic State (IS), it is also one of the Syrian towns most severely affected by the war.

Three years earlier, in 2018, the Lebanon/France/Turkey-based duo Boshoco, a name paying homage to an ice cream popular in their hometown of Aleppo in the 1990s, released an hour-long remix on SoundCloud whose title, 'Chapter C: Route Athrya-Khanasir', refers to a road that runs between two small towns that are located in Aleppo's south-eastern hinterlands and that was heavily fought over by oppositional groups, IS-fighters and Syrian regime

---

[42] www.shkoon.bandcamp.com/album/rima.

[43] For more on the practice of 'cultural recycling', see Martin 2008. For a discussion of the history and aesthetics of remix and sampling cultures, see Navas 2012. For a collection of essays in which artists from around the world describe their digital sampling techniques in their own words, see Miller 2008. On the specific role of sampling within (underground) electronic music scenes, see Rodgers 2003.

Figure 5 Cover art for 'Moniety' (2021) Courtesy of Nakriz and Bashar Salloum.[44]

forces. A reference to Aleppo appears in the subtitle of the song. In it, they describes the nature of the musical 'trip' that they envision, drawing on a line from an Aleppian song that, famously sung by Sabah Fakhri, describes a path 'surrounded by olive trees [*killu sajr zeitouni*]'. In their version, 'the road to Aleppo that I walked on [*darab ḥalab yelli mashitu*]', becomes 'the road to Aleppo that I dreamed of [*darab ḥalab yelli ḥalamtu*]', a road that they render through a hybrid texture of sounds: deep house rhythms, the theme music from David Lynch's iconic *Twin Peaks* television series, French hip-hop, samples of a *taqsim* (instrumental improvisation) and a *layali* (vocal improvisation on the words '*ya layl*', 'O night') and the disjointed shouts of street vendors, honking cars, mooing cows and bleating sheep. Boshoco's 'Chapter C: Route Athrya-Khanasir' sounds out a path of return to a city that has come to reside in people's minds. 'What a trip . . . Really takes you to back to the streets of Syria' is how one online listener responded to the song.[45]

What emerges from this brief and necessarily incomplete overview of Syrian sampling practices, then, is a map of musical networks and cross-fertilization that extends across place and time. This map testifies to the global circulation of digitalised Arab music, sounds and media content; it reveals the migratory paths

---

[44] www.youtube.com/watch?v=ots4uwi0qZQ.
[45] https://soundcloud.com/boshoco/chapter-c-khanasir.

of displaced Syrian musicians, connecting them not only to the urban centres and transnational music scenes of the Arab world's diaspora but also, importantly, to the places they left behind; and it gives insights into the ways in which local and regional musical aesthetics such as *tarab* live on in new, experimental and *virtual* contexts.

As vividly illustrated in the 'Shahba' video and Hello Psychaleppo's self-portrait of being confined to the armchair in front of his television, electro-tarab emerged at a time in which displaced Syrians across the world found large parts of their (musical) lives operating online, or as expressed by Syrian artist Khaled Barakeh (2014: 158), in Syria's 'virtual "parallel republic"'. Enabling individuals to upload, share and (live) comment on music, video-clips, images and media content, the Internet has led to new forms of musical sociality (see also Nooshin's (2018) discussion of online music cultures in Iran). A main operator of this sociality, and an important site for connecting people's private musical worlds, has been the music platform SoundCloud, an online streaming service that has lent itself to the DIY cultures of independent musicians around the world.[46] Almost all of the previously mentioned Syrian/Arab electronic musicians and songs can be found there, including Hello Psychaleppo's song 'Tarab Dub', one of his most popular tracks; as of October 2022, this had been listened to more than 690,000 times.[47] The song is composed around a sample of the song '*Min yelli qal in al-qamr yeshbih limaḥbub al-fu'ad* [Who Said That the Moon Compares to the Beloved Heart]', a *dawr* (precomposed vocal form especially popular in late nineteenth and early twentieth century Egypt) originally composed by the Egyptian Zakkaria Ahmed (1896–1961) and performed by the legendary Um Kalthoum. From 'much love from Amman' to the statement 'more Arabian culture is needed in the West', to someone praising Hello Psychaleppo in a typically Egyptian vernacular '*Enta Prince* [you are a prince!]', the online reactions that the song has provoked provide a sense of the different, trans-national and virtual worlds that the song and its sample traverse. Most importantly, and owing to the function that allows people to leave a comment at the precise second of a song, such fan responses have come to substitute the live exclamations of the sammiʻah: 'Ye leyyyyyyyyllll', 'Allaaah' and 'Uuuuuf!' is how Hello Psychaleppo's fans have expressed their appreciation, and these virtual signs of affection are often followed by comments in which people ask for the name of the original sample or share the songs' lyrics: '*Wal kun yenawwar bil-ʻam* [the universe is illuminated by the

---

[46] See Nickell 2020 for more on the use of SoundCloud among independent musicians in Lebanon.
[47] https://soundcloud.com/hellopsychaleppo/tarab-dub.

moon]' or ' . . . *ama al-ḥabib nur al-'ayun* [. . . but the l loved one is the light of the eyes!]'.

A particularly insightful and visual response to 'Tarab Dub' came from the Syrian graphic designer Omar Shammah. From his new hometown of Augsburg in Germany, he explained to me how, listening to the song for the first time, he had remembered his grandparents' neighbourhood in Aleppo:

> I just closed my eyes and listened to it and I was suddenly walking in an old poor alley. A very quiet one though, which is pretty unusual in these neigh-bourhoods. It was dream-like . . . I then opened my eyes to capture that atmosphere on paper.[48]

The resulting artwork (Figure 6) relates the intimacy of people's private and virtual listening experiences with a collective experience of displacement: a world of houses that look like shattered TVs, illuminated by the moon that Um Kalthoum sings about. Despite the grim reality that it depicts, the image also registers a hope in music being able to sustain a sense of home in times of war and displacement. One notices how this image, again, contains ribbons, ribbons which one may interpret as symbolising people's affective and musical attachments to their lost homes (and TVs screens) and which uplift and tie together a community of listeners.

3.3 Lost Homes: Music, Memory and Pleasure

Omar Shammah's visualisation of Hello Psychaleppo's 'Tarab Dub' powerfully illustrates how displaced Syrians have linked tarab to their country's recent history of war. Indeed, in a struggle to find words to express the sorrows that this war has generated, some Syrians have referred me to songs. 'If I only knew how my beloved ones are, on which lands they have settled to stay, I swear, I did not choose this separation, but these days have judged it upon me [*ya leyta sha 'ri kayfa ḥalu aḥibati, wa bi eyya arḍin khayyamu wa aqamu, wallahi ma ikhtartu al-firaqa wa lakin ḥakkamat 'aleyya bi dhalik al-ayyam*]': this poetic text of a famous *mawwal* (non-metred and improvised sung poetry) was quoted to me to express the pain of being separated from one's friends and loved ones. In a similar vein, Egyptian singer Abd al-Wahhab's song '*Ya musafir waḥdak* [O Lonesome Traveller]' has for some become a means of mediating their memory of migrating to Europe. The Berlin-based Aleppian singer Abdallah Rahhal, for example, recounted singing this song when he was held up by state authorities on his journey through Eastern Europe. He also explained that to him, the lyrics of Lebanese singer Melham Barakat's '*Ya ḥubbi yelli ghab* [O my love who

---

[48] Written correspondence (in English), 5 March 2019.

TARAB DUB

50 X 70 cm,
Charcoal, and Ink on Drawing Paper

Figure 6 *Tarab Dub* Courtesy of Omar Shammah

vanished]', where it declares 'After you for whom do the flowers bow? After you for whom does your sun shine, my world? [*min b'adek la min al-zahr byenḥani wa tasharaq la min shamsek ya dini*]' no longer spoke about an absent lover but expressed the collective sorrow over a lost homeland.[49] A similar sentiment was evoked by one of Rahhal's fans, also a former resident of Aleppo. Only recently, so he told me, and after having been forced to leave his home-town, had he come to understand and be affected by the meaning of the Iraqi mawwal that proclaims: 'The one who has lost a loved one may forget them after a year. The one who has lost gold will find it on the gold market. But the one who has lost their homeland – where will they find it [*yelli mudi'a muḥib yomkin sannah wa yensahu, yelli mudi'a al-dhahab bisuq al-dhahab yelgah, bas yelli mudi'a al-watan waen al-watan yelgah*]?'[50]

---

[49] Personal conversation, 16 September 2016.   [50] Personal conversation, 25 September 2016.

Experiencing a history of displacement as a 'lonesome lover' and 'vanishing love' and being affected by a previously unintelligible evocation of a 'lost homeland' through the memory of one's own loss – accounts like these bring to the fore the multiple and personal meanings that Syrians have attached to local and regional tarab songs by associating them with their country's recent history. Some musicians have taken such associations a step further. An example are Nihad Alabsi and Philippe Antoine Zarif, who make up the already mentioned duo Boshoco. Like Hello Psychaleppo, they too are from Aleppo and they have also rhetorically evoked the concept of tarab when describing their music as 'made to bring joy through dance: the sublime natural high known in Arabic as "*saltaneh*"',[51] a term that, like tarab, denotes a state of creative musical ecstasy and enchantment. And they too have used samples to reference their hometown's recent violent history. One of their most popular deep house (a subgenre of house music) tracks, '*Ard'diyar*' ('ard' translates as 'ground', 'earth' or 'land', and 'diyar' is the name for a traditional Arabic house) samples a scene that was originally part of the Al-Jazeera documentary 'Death of Aleppo' (Anon., 2015). In it, the well-known Aleppian chanter Sheikh Ahmed Habboush can be seen walking through the ruins of his house while singing a mawwal that addresses his destroyed home as a departed lover 'whose love remained in his heart [*lam yab 'ud 'an al-qalb ḥubukum*]'.[52] When I asked Boshoco why they choose to sample this particular song, they responded that they felt that the scene of someone lamenting their shattered home articulated a 'collective condition', 'the condition of Aleppo', as they put it. They went on:

> We wanted to turn it into something joyful, into something people could dance to, into its opposite, in a way. That's why we merged it with deep house. We wanted this condition to be present in moments where people are happy, when people dance, when they don't associate it with something sad.[53]

To some, smoothening out the memory of someone's ruined home into a generalised mode of musical ecstasy may offer evidence of the defusing seductions of a clubbing culture and the aesthetic imperatives of a dancing elite. To some, it may even give credit to the kind of negative views on tarab culture that Jonathan Shannon (2006: 185) has documented in his monograph on music in Syria, including criticism of it as 'emotional escapism' from reality and a sign of political passiveness in times of national struggle.[54]

---

[51] www.soundcloud.com/boshoco/arddyar-original-mix.

[52] https://youtu.be/rIfscgdRhbk?t=1861.   [53] Skype interview [in English], 18 January 2017.

[54] According to Shannon (2006: 185), this critique goes so far that some people claim that the 1967 war with Israel was lost because all Arabs were 'high [*matrub*]' from listening to Um Kalthoum.

Boshoco's comment, together with social media content that suggests that they have recently been able return to make music in Aleppo while the sampled Sheikh Habboush, as one of the few musicians who openly aligned himself with the city's oppositional forces, is probably unlikely to return in the near future, may indeed serve as an example of a society torn apart by war, separated not only by frontlines but divided into those who left/are unable to return and those who stayed/are able to return. Such a view, I argue, must be complexified through a reading that maps 'displacement' onto spaces that go beyond the material.[55]

An example of such a view in the context of music is provided by Nadeem Karkabi's (2020) recent study of Palestinian rave scenes in Israel. His analysis of the mobilisation of musical and hedonistic pleasure as a mode of self-liberation (*taharrur*) from a state that seems to offer Palestinians no alternative to being either a 'complicit' or a 'resistant' national subject (682), may serve as an explanation for the role evocations of musical ecstasy such as the quote from Boshoco play in a context in which many Syrians have found themselves neither engaged in revolutionary action, nor actively supporting the Syrian regime, but united instead by the wish to temporarily suspend the pressures of asserting their political belonging and engage in all the pleasurable seductions that dance, musical consumption and night life culture have to offer.

The following and final section will provide insights into this world via ethnographic snapshots of a Hello Psychaleppo concert that I attended in Beirut in November 2016, the month in which the Syrian regime's offensive on East Aleppo entered its final stage. This was a time when tens of thousands of residents, especially those associated with Aleppo's opposition, were forced to flee their homes and when 'any given day', as I am reminded by my fieldnotes, 'exemplified the ongoing tragedy'. By the end of the following month, regime forces will have taken back Aleppo, causing thousands of people not only to lose their homes but also their right to return. As we shall see, the different samples that formed part of Hello Psychaleppo's concert that night will lead us back to Aleppo, associating it with the mythologised 'city of music', the loss of land and once again with musical pleasure.

---

[55] Such a reading has recently been explicated by Georgina Ramsay and Hedda Haugen Askland in their article 'Displacement as Condition: A Refugee, a Farmer and the Teleology of Life' (2022). Their work connects to studies that have mobilised ethnographic approaches to gain insights into the experiences of displaced people that go beyond mainstream humanitarian discourses that frame their lives exclusively in terms of trauma and victimhood (Cabot 2016; Chatty 2014, 2017; Lacroix and Fiddian-Qasmiyeh 2013; Sigona 2014).

4 'Radio Beirut': Samples as Codes

Radio Beirut, a former hub of Lebanon's alternative music scene, used to be located on Rue Armenia in Beirut's hip Gemeizzeh neighbourhood.[56] Frequented by Syrian refugee children selling roses, craft-beer-drinking hipsters and white Mercedes jeeps carrying members of the Lebanese upper class, this street is not only one of the hotspots of Beirut nightlife, it is also a reminder of the societal rifts that mark Lebanese society. When I arrive at the doors, I find the outside windows covered in flyers (Figure 7) promoting tonight's electro-tarab live set for an entrance fee that in November 2016 was equivalent to roughly £7.50.[57] And I note that the advertisement for tonight's concert uses the same image of the yellow man that flashed up at the end of the 'Shahba' video, only this time there are three of them, not one.

The majority of attendees are in their 20s and 30s. Present are Radio Beirut's core fan group, members of Lebanon's vibrant hip-hop scene and a number of foreigners, including students from a nearby Arabic language school, humanitarian workers and journalists based in Beirut, American Lebanese AUB students who spend time in the country to study and reconnect with their roots, and a significant number of Syrians. A group of friends have come all the way from Damascus and will go back tomorrow to a city that they describe to me as being 'so safe that it is strange'. Lamenting the kind of paralysis that has befallen the residents of a city surrounded by war, one of them will later remark: 'I sleep more than nine hours every night. People have become very lazy … this laziness [*al-kasl*] is everywhere.' A few of the other Syrians are from the southern Hauran region. They have moved to Lebanon to escape Syrian military service and will not be able to return to their country any time soon. And then there are Syrians who are back for a visit but have started a new life elsewhere, outside the Middle East – people like Eldahr. Just as those who make up the audience of Radio Beirut come from different (even if largely urban middle class) backgrounds, Beirut, as I learned while living in the city from 2011–12 carries a multitude of meanings. A city still coming to terms with its own war-raged past, a civil war that lasted from 1975 to 1990; both 'gateway' to and 'get-away' from the Middle East; home to be re-discovered; place of long-term exile; refuge from the horrors of the Syrian war and a place of (artistic) promise and possibilities, to name but a few.

---

[56] Launched in 2012 by Jihad Samhat, a former bomb disposal officer of the United Nations Mine Action Service, the physical live venue of Radio Beirut, according to a statement on its social media page, was forced to close down in 2020 as a result of the Covid pandemic.

[57] A sum that is significantly lower than, for example, the concerts of Aleppian singer Muhammad Khairy, that, in 2016, regularly took place at the 'Theatro Verdun', a cabaret-style music venue in the basement of a giant shopping mall on the other side of town. There, tickets cost roughly £25, and require the purchase of a dinner. In financial terms, tonight's event is far from representing the high-end of Lebanese society.

Music and the City

Figure 7 Advertisement for Hello Pschaleppo's concert in Beirut,
12 November 2016 Courtesy of Samer Saem Eldahr.

Most importantly, for many Syrians, and arguably within the Arab diasporic
imagination in general, Beirut has become a place of 'in-between'. On the one
hand, the city continues to maintain its historical status as a cosmopolitan and
liberal cultural hub, seemingly distant from the more conservative and now war-
ravaged Syria. But on the other, in light of the mass migration movements to
Turkey, Europe and beyond, this distance has collapsed and Beirut has become
the place of 'those who stayed'. And what about Aleppo?

4.1 'Tabaluj al-Subḥ': Paths of Return

A dark, ambient drone, interspersed with the sound of chirping birds marks the
beginning of the concert.[58] Resonating amid the background noise and people's
chatter at the bar are the highly distorted fragments from a recording of a non-
metrical *madīḥ*, a song in praise of the prophet Muhammad, as it was once
recited live by the Aleppian religious singer Adeeb al-Dayekh (1938–2001).[59]

---

[58] A recording of the full concert was uploaded by Radio Beirut on YouTube:
https://youtu.be/SOoaGo_drk0. When discussing individual samples used in the concert, I will
provide the link with the corresponding time-specific URL.

[59] Al-Dayekh is widely recognised as Aleppo's foremost singer of the mawwal and, as a former
member of the al-Kindi ensemble of Syrian sacred music, he is featured on numerous recordings
and has participated in several international festivals (see Poché 2001: 566; Shannon 2003b).

Eventually, his voice articulates the first clear verse: '*Tabaluj al-subḥ, tabaluj al-subḥu faltanẓur lahu al-muqalu wa ussisa lahu al-ʿadlu faltakhdaʿ lahu al-midadu* [dawn has broken, so let the eyes behold, justice has been established for him, so let all beings submit].'[60]

'*Ya ḥabibi ya ʿayni!* [My love, my eye!]' – 'Ahh!' – '*Ruḥi! Yallah!* [Go!]', '*Na ʿam, na ʿam!* [Yes!]'. On the original sample, one hears the encouraging voices of al-Dayekh's sammiʿah-audience, prompting him to repeat the verse again until everyone bursts into a long, ecstatic and collectively iterated '*Allah*', and the singer moves on with the next verse: '*Wa ahshraqat shamsu hadin fastada' biha kull al-baraya wa ʿam al-unsu wa al-jadhalu fastada' biha* [The sun of the guide has shone and all of creation has been enlightened, a sense of companionship and cheerfulness prevailed]' The drone, which until now held the tonic of the *maqam* in a way reminiscent of a traditional *oud or qanun* accompaniment, changes register. For a brief moment the minor chords and al-Dayekh's weeping voice stir up a sense of grief and sorrow often referred to as *ḥuzn* in Arabic, an aesthetic quality intimately linked to the realm of Quranic recitation where it is believed to serve as a catalyst for religious experience by softening the listeners' hearts and moving them to tears (Nelson 1985: 89–100).[61] This ecstatic effect is heightened by the extensive reverb effect (very common more generally in the music of the region) that Hello Psychaleppo has used to overlay al-Dayekh's voice as well as the shouts and sighs from the audience members heard on the original recording. '*Ya ʿayni ʿala al-ḥabib!* [My eye upon the beloved!]', one of them exclaims enthusiastically, and al-Dayekh repeats: '*Wa ahshraqat shamsu hadin fastada' biha kull al-baraya wa ʿam al-unsu wa al-jadhalu fastada' . . . .*' This time, the verse is suspended halfway. Haunted by arpeggio drones, al-Dayekh's voice dissolves into a chromatic scale that, picked up by Hello Psychaleppo on his midi keyboard, eventually makes way for the insetting beat, and the crowd at Radio Beirut starts to dance.

In his book chapter, 'Nightingales and Sweet Basil – The Cultural Geography of Aleppine Song', Jonathan Shannon has taken up the question of what it means to 'listen' to Aleppo. Besides providing the reader with a now invaluable memory of the soundscape of the city's old town in the years just prior to the outbreak of the war, Shannon proposes listening to the city's local repertoire of *qudud* and the naturalistic metaphors and imaginary they evoke 'architecturally'. He writes:

> ....explicit and implicit and explicit associations between place and sound arise
> less from fundamental structural similarities in the domains of music and

---

[60] This is a rough translation of a complex poetic text. I thank Ahmed al-Khashem for his guidance.

[61] For an exploration of the centrality of the idea of *ḥuzn* and its Syriac equivalent *ḥasho* in the musical and religious experience of Aleppo's Syriac communities, see Jarjour 2018. For a study of its Turkish equivalent, *hüzün*, see Gill 2017.

architecture, even when they may exist, than from the metonymic role of the old city as an index of tradition and cultural authenticity. Affectively, the older songs and styles evoke an older way of being in the world, one associated more with quarters of the old city than with the new. (Shannon 2018:153)

Hello Psychaleppo's sampling of Adeeb al-Dayekh and his live audience allows one to draw similar connections between sound and place, albeit on a micro-level. Whoever is familiar with this rendition of the *madih*, willing to excavate the sample's original recording from YouTube[62] or engage Tricia Rose's (1994: 116) characterisation of sampling as 'musical time machine' will find themselves in the past. There, Adeeb al-Dayekh continues to sing in praise of the prophet, about his birth being the reason for Arabs to be proud (*iftakhiru*), celebrate (*ihtafilu*) and express their collective yearning (*shawq*) for a return of the time when the second caliph of Islam, Omar Ibn al-Khattab, erected 'a castle of glory [*majid*] that the heroes of Europe could not compete with, whatever their efforts [*mahma lahu badhalu*]'. Such verses are sealed with the joint response by an audience of pious listeners: 'God bless our prophet Muhammad and grant him salvation [*sall allahu 'ala sayydna muhammad salla allahu 'alyhi wa sallam*]!'

The sampled *madih* not only echoes Islamic history; it also takes us back to Aleppo, this time into the neighbourhood south of Bab al-Hadid ('The Iron Gate'), one of the city's historic gates. This area is home to the Kiltawiyyah mosque and its adjacent *madrasah* (religious school), one of the main centres of Adeeb al-Dhayekh's musical activities. Built in the thirteenth century CE, the mosque was damaged during the Syrian war and, according to Syrian state media, the shrine of the Sufi Sheikh and public educator Sheikh Muhammad Nabhan, who founded the *madrasah* in the 1960s destroyed by radical Islamic groups.[63] With Adeeb al-Dayekh having died in 2001 and with much of the traditional urban environment he operated in having been damaged or destroyed by war, what the loudspeakers carry onto the dancefloor in Beirut, then, is a memory of an Aleppo that as such no longer exists. Perhaps the opening sample will have reminded some of tonight's attendees, especially those who refer to Aleppo as a place of familiarity and emotional, cultural and/or musical identification, of a home that feels much closer than the approximately 400 kilometres that separate Aleppo from Beirut on the map. But the introduction to the concert only lasts a couple of minutes. What follows gives a sense of the physical and social distance that separates the scene that the original sample of Adeeb al-Dayekh evoked (a religious chanter surrounded by an audience of pious listeners) from electro-tarab's present context: Eldahr, laughing, holding

---

[62] www.youtube.com/watch?v=vfHPH7gRWxk.
[63] https://www.sana.sy/en/?p=25426. As pictures shared on social media document, the musical and religious activities at the Kiltawiyya mosque have since resumed.

up his fist and moving between his laptop and midi keyboard; a pounding beat that eventually accelerates to over 150 bpm; flickering visuals and animated characters on a screen behind the dancefloor; loudspeakers that blast out the echoing call '*Ta 'ali* [Come to me]'; sound effects that draw the listener into the 'infinite noise spirals' characteristic of psytrance music (Rietveld 2011); and a dancing crowd that, surrounded by walls that feature murals of the American singer Prince as well as Fairouz (b. 1934) and her son Ziad Rahbani (b. 1956) – two of Lebanon's most iconic musicians[64] – raves in synchronised baby steps similar to those seen at Berlin techno-parties.

Framed around the song '*Fog Alghaim* [Above the Clouds]',[65] the next twenty minutes render electro-tarab as a form of music in which a memory of Aleppo gives way to a sound that, more than that of al-Dayekh, Sabah Fakhri or any of the previously mentioned Aleppian musicians, has reminded fans of the kind of extra-terrestrial 'space travel' typical of psytrance music (see St John 2013). 'This is alien abduction!' is how one listener commented on the song's studio version online,[66] while another associated it with the music of the Israeli psytrance duo Infected Mushroom. Eldahr himself described the process of altering vocal samples to an extent that their sonority takes precedence over their verbal meaning as 'going abstract'.[67] If, previously, the use of samples acted as an homage to one of Aleppo's most distinguished musicians, their distortion into unrecognisable sonic fragments seems to sound out a rupture with precisely the past that his music refers to. Perhaps one could compare the social effect of this distortion to what Christopher Stone has observed with regard to Ziad Rahbani, the iconic Lebanese musician and composer whose mural is depicted on the walls of Radio Beirut and whose career also developed against the background of a war. According to Stone (2007: 2), Rahbani not only celebrated the musical diversity of Lebanon but also 'disabused' its audience of nostalgia for a pre-civil war Lebanon. Perhaps one could also think of distortion as a way of preserving a pre-war memory from being 'abused' by the present, in the sense evoked by 'Refugee A', a Syrian electronic musician now based in Vienna, one of whose songs also includes a sample of Adeeb al-Dayekh. According to him, the current generation of Syrians was 'unworthy' of the older musicians' words and their sincerity, because of their entanglement in the horrors of war. He explained:

> The difference between us now and the time of Adeeb al-Dayekh is huge. At
> that time people were honest and kind, today it's not like this. . . . If this music
> and the lyrics that we listen to by Adeeb al-Dayekh were really expressing us,

---

[64] For an exploration of their role in modern Lebanese history, see Stone 2007.

[65] https://youtu.be/SOoaGo_drk0?t=832.

[66] www.soundcloud.com/hellopsychaleppo/01-fog-alghaim.

[67] Personal conversation, 16 November 2016.

right now we were not in the midst of this war. We would not have war. We are
not like this, we are liars. Everyone only cares about himself and about no one
else. . . .. A war does not happen out of nowhere, there are reasons for this and
one of the reasons is that we are a society of liars. What Adeeb al-Dayekh
sings is really sincere, it really comes from the inside. . . . Maybe we dream of
the old days, long before the war, when everything was all right. It was all
right. Maybe we dream. Maybe this is also a reason that we want to go back.
But that's over. People won't be able to return; the country is gone.[68]

Distortion as a way of sounding out the devastating reality of an impossible
return? While such an interpretation remains purely speculative, Hello
Psychaleppo himself directly refers to this reality with a sample that disrupts
the couple of minutes 'above the clouds'. Instead of leading us back to the old
town of Aleppo, it transmits a poetic text that activates a memory of Aleppo's
recent violent history, linking the city to a Palestinian experience of displacement.

4.2 'Ya Ard': From Aleppo to Palestine

Back on the dancefloor, the music fades out. Left is the voice of the late Palestinian
singer and poet Abu Arab (1931–2014), reciting a poem about the Palestinian
national struggle:

> O Land, your people are 'Neshama'[69]/ O Land, your people are 'Neshama' /
> old men to young girls / have stepped on your path and sacrificed / they do not
> fear death / every house and every street / every church and every mosque / is
> roaring and the universe is listening / to a voice louder than cannons / I heard
> Taha[70] call out / and the voice of Jesus in the cave / stone the devil[71], my
> people / how we endured our fate / patience is no longer useful / be our
> witness, world / be our witness and the universe will see / see your people / in
> their cities and villages / waves are rising in the (refugee) camps / they broke
> the chests of the youth / but my people's will won't be broken / they destroyed
> orphanages / but my people persevered / they were not destroyed / the whole

---

[68] Skype conversation, 21 December 2016.

[69] The term *'Neshama'* is difficult to translate. Bearing connotations of Arab masculinity, and
commonly associated with Bedouin, equestrian and desert culture, it may best be rendered as
a combination of resilience, steadfastness, courageousness, dignity and generosity. Throughout
the Syrian revolution, the expression seems to have gained new prominence. It served, for
example, as the title of a 2012 album by Syrian musician and composer Wael al-Qaq. According
to him, the expression was evoked by Syrian activists to set themselves in opposition to the
regime's paramilitary thugs, the *'shabiḥa* [ghosts]' (personal conversation, 10 August 2013).

[70] 'Taha' is one of the names of the prophet Muhammad.

[71] The 'stoning of the devil' represents one of a series of rituals performed during the Islamic
pilgrimage to Mecca, where pilgrims throw stones at three walls located in Mina, just east of
Mekka. Here, the image of stone-throwing probably also serves as a reference to a common
Palestinian practice of resisting Israeli military and occupation, a practice that was especially
prevalent during the first Palestinian Intifada (1987–93).

world is witnessing / my people, more patient than Ayyoub[72] / I heard Taha call out / justice rolled up its sleeves / and Ali held Zulfiqar[73] in his hand / and Haider pulled out the 'edge of the sword'[74] / and the virgin Mary called out / O Jerusalem, God is Great!

Ya ard, ahlek neshama / Ya ard, ahlek neshama / min kuhul wa min sabaya / mishu fi darbek daḥaya / ma yehabun al-manaya / kul bayt wa kul shariʿa / kul kanisseh wa kul jamʿa / yuhduru wa al-kun samʿa / wa bisawt aqwa min al-madafʿa / wa smaʿt taha yunadi / wa sawt ʿissa bil-mugharah / urjumu iblis ya ahli / kam sabarna ʿala qadarna / wa al-sabr ma ʿad nafʿa / ishhadi ya dunya ʿana / ishhadi wal-koun yishhad / shuf ahlak / fi mudunhum fi qurahum / mukhayamati muj tzkhar / kasaru duluʿal-shabab / wa shaʿbi ʿazmu ma tkassar / damaru buyut al-yatama / wa shaʿbi samid ma itdhamar / kul ha-dunya tishhad / wa shaʿbi min ayub asbar / wa smʿat taha yunadi / wa ʿan zunud al haqq nhamar / wa ʿali, ʿali dllu al-fiyyat fi ldu / wu ʙul ḥad as-sayl ḥaidar / wa mariam al-ʿadhra' saḥet / ya quds allahu akbar[75]

Born in a village in the Galilee in Mandatory Palestine in 1931, Abu Arab, whose real name was Ibrahim Muhammad Salih, became a refugee in 1948. This year, known in Palestinian memory as *al-Nakba*, 'the catastrophe', marked the establishment of the modern state of Israel, the first Arab-Israeli war and the expulsion and displacement of around 750,000 Palestinians (see Morris 2008; Saʾdi and Abu-Lughod 2007). Joining around 100,000 Palestinians who had fled to Syria in the aftermath of 1948 (al-Hardan 2016: 5; see also Gabiam 2016) and after first residing in Beirut, Abu Arab eventually settled in Syria, where he reportedly died in 2014. As a performer of numerous protest songs, Abu Arab plays an important role in the popular memory of Palestinian resistance. Combining colloquial poetry with popular/folkloric (*shaʿbi*) musical forms, the songs he is known for have memorialised important events in Palestinian history: they have addressed exiled Palestinians, those residing within the borders of Israel (also referred to as '48 Palestinians) and those living under occupation in the West Bank and Gaza, and they have celebrated the various guerrilla groups that, from the 1960s, fought for national Palestinian liberation. By the late 1970s, the dissemination of Abu Arab's songs and poems via cheap cassette tapes meant that they could be heard in Palestinian camp households across the West Bank, Gaza, Jordan, Lebanon and Syria (Massad 2003: 31–32; McDonald 2013: 101–103).

---

[72] A central figure in all Abrahamic religions and considered a prophet in Islam, Ayyoub/Job endures years of suffering and afflictions sent upon him by the devil, thereby proving his steadfastness to God.

[73] According to Islamic belief, 'Zulfiqar' is the name of the sword which the fourth Caliph Ali received from Muhammad.

[74] Haider (lion) is a name attributed to Caliph Ali, but this verse may possibly also be a reference to the poem '*qabbaltu khad as-sayf* [I kissed the cheek of the sword]' by Jordan-based Palestinian writer and politician Haider Mahmoud (b. 1942).

[75] https://youtu.be/SOoaGo_drk0?t=1554. For the sample's original, see https://youtu.be/x0CmnBPjDRQ.

The strophes that Hello Psychaleppo has sampled in his song 'Ya Ard' stem from this corpus of poetry. Replete with religious imagery that evokes solidarity between Palestinian Christians and Muslims, mourns the victims of an ongoing history of displacement and celebrates key tropes in the Palestinian national struggle – *al-sumud* (steadfastness) and *sabr* (patience) – Abu Arab's verses register a homeland that lives on (and is fought for) via the embodied memory of its former communities. Tonight, these themes, together with the poem's call for resilience and redemption, all of which were 'hallmarks of indigenous folk song following 1948' (McDonald 2013: 103) no longer refer only to the Palestinian experience.

'I'm like a Palestinian who left with the keys to their home – expecting to use them again.'[76] This is how Eldahr associated his own experience of displacement with the memory of the Palestinian *Nakba*. Doing so, he mobilised one of the iconic objects of Palestinian memory and a symbol of a future return: the key that many displaced Palestinians kept to the houses they were forced to abandon in 1948.[77] This bond between Aleppo and Palestine had already been evoked by others: 'From Aleppo to Gaza runs a river of blood [*min ḥalab ila ghazzah nahr dam jari*]', read the banners that Syrian protesters held up during anti-regime demonstrations in Aleppo in 2014, protesters who were already referred to in revolutionary discourse as '*al-samideen*' (from *al-sumud*, 'steadfastness', a central Palestinian trope, as mentioned).[78] A year earlier, during a ceremony that marked the second anniversary of the Syrian uprising, the '48 Palestinian singer and activist Rim al-Banna (1966–2018) identified Syrians' plight with a Palestinian history of suffering at a time when much of the Arab world seemed to show nothing but disavowal. Dressed in a *Kufiya* (Palestinian scarf and headcover) and positioned in front of a music stand covered with the Syrian revolutionary flag, she presented a Syrian interpretation of the Palestinian nationalist song "*habbat al-nar* [The fire has swollen]" (see McDonald 2013: 106; 294) that included the following verses: 'The fire has swollen from Idlib to Aleppo/They bombed the streets with barrel bombs/Millions were displaced and nobody from the Arabs felt the pain, except the Palestinian [*Habbat al-nar min idlib la ḥalab/qasafu ḥarat bil-baramil darab/ sharrad malayin wa ma ḥada min al-ʿarab ḥasis bil-jurḥ ghayr al-falistini*].'[79]

---

[76] www.alaraby.co.uk/english/society/2017/3/17/hello-psychaleppo-the-world-is-pretty-surreal-right-now.

[77] Other iconic objects of Palestinian memory include images of olive trees, oranges, rural stone houses and traditional embroidered dresses (see Khalili 2007: 6; Swedenburg 1990).

[78] www.creativememory.org/en/archives/65468/from-aleppo-to-gaza/.

[79] www.youtube.com/watch?time_continue=171&v=F2RgdU3J8jc.

In 2016, during the Syrian regime's final offensive on oppositional-held East Aleppo and the forced population transfers, residents of besieged neighbourhoods sought comfort in songs previously associated with Palestinian history. For instance, on 15 December, Marwa and Saleh, a young couple who reportedly married during the war, shared an image of themselves in a neighbourhood in East Aleppo that captured their last message before leaving their hometown in the convoy of refugees. Holding each other in their arms, he carrying a weapon over his shoulder, she holding a spray can, they faced the wall of a house onto which they had graffitied '*Raja 'in ya hawa* [We are coming back, love]', the title of a song that, composed by the Rahbani brothers, was first performed by Fairouz in the musical play 'Lulu' (1974) and is, like many other of her songs, dedicated to the Palestinian cause.[80] At around the same time, a folk song, the lyrics of which were once dedicated to Aitat, a Lebanese village and former centre of the Palestinian insurgency during the Lebanese War and the Palestinian-Israeli conflict in the 1980s, became one of the 'anthems' of Aleppo's besieged and displaced residents: 'On the road to Aleppo, they cut my prayers [*'ala tariq ḥalab yummi qata 'u salati*]'. This is how its refrain captured people's shattered hopes for a better future, while condemning the indifference of those who were celebrating the return of Aleppo to the Syrian State: 'Whoever dances and is joyful beside me, is waiting for my death [*yelli yefraḥ yur'us yummi natir mamati*]'. Associating Aleppo's destruction not with Dresden towards the end of the Second World War or Sarajevo in the 1990s – comparisons that were frequently drawn in global media outlets at the time – but with the historic erasure of Palestinian villages and towns, these forms of cultural expressions are examples of how Palestinian history has re-entered the Syrian imagination in ways that rest on a shared experience of displacement.[81] In other words, it is as if a Palestinian culture of grief and resilience, having found its way into popular Syrian memory via Arab nationalist thought, mass media and the approximately 560,000 Palestinians that, before 2011, were residing in Syria, has come to *stand in* for narrating the traumas of a war that Syrians have yet to come to terms with.

The resonance of 'Ya Ard' in a Beirut nightclub, then, not only testifies to the active memory of Palestinian protest songs across the Arab world, it also becomes a commentary on Syrians' experience of displacement. However, as

---

[80] For a study of the central role Fairouz and the Rahbani brothers have played in producing songs dedicated to the Palestinian struggle, especially following the 1967 war, see Massad 2003 and Stone 2008.

[81] For studies on how a socially transformed memory of the *nakba* has led to the formation of new political subjectivities among Syrian Palestinians in the course of the Syrian uprising and war, see al-Hardan 2016; Jasim 2016; al-Khateeb, Rollins and Shaheen 2020.

the next sample will demonstrate, Hello Psychaleppo is also concerned with temporarily replacing such political realities with a state of musical and convivial pleasure.

4.3 'Urqsu!': From Displacement to the Yellow Man

Back in Radio Beirut, Abu Arab's voice has been reduced to fragments, interspersed with a pounding beat and the sounds of alarming, distorted sirens. People resume dancing, with some moving as if enacting the poem's declaration of resilience: '*Ya ard nahna sakhrek* [O Land, we are your rocks]'. A girl grabs her hair, while stamping her feet on the dancefloor. '*Ya ard nahna sakhrek wan-nabat* [O Land, we are your rocks and your plants]'. The person next to her pulls his shirt over his head, covering his face and swaying his body back and forth. '*Utlubina, tujadina, tujadi mina al-thabat* [Call us, you will find us steady].' Soon, a new voice resonates over the dancefloor, presenting the audience with the following message (in Arabic):

> Youth! Make yourself comfortable in any place! Dance, sing, stay up late, live in high spirits! Dance! Dance, sing and rejoice! You must sing, dance and be ready! Sing, dance, and be prepared! . . . These are high morals! Take a look, Europe! Take a look, America! [*Ayyuha al-shabab, khudhu rahatkum bi ay makan! Urqsu, ghannu, asharu, 'aishu bi al-ruh al-ma'nawiyyah al-'aliyah! Urqsu! Urqsu wa ghannu, wa afrahu wa amrahu! 'Alayykum an tughannu wa turqusu wa tast'addu! Ghannu, wa arqsu wa ast'addu! Hadhihi al-ruh al-ma'nawiyyah al-'aliyah! . . . Unzur ya europa! Unzur ya amrika!*][82]

Calling on people to sing, dance, rejoice and make themselves comfortable *in any place* (and under the gaze of the American and European community), this sample can be understood as a meta-commentary on what is perhaps the main motivation for Hello Psychaleppo's reactivation of Aleppo's musical-mythic legacy: the production of a distinctively Arab style of electronic dance music as well as the experience of musical pleasure (tarab) in times of displacement. Yet the sample also helps to point out that in times when many of electro-tarab's constituencies find themselves dispersed around the world, such musical pleasure may first and foremost consist in a shared sense of home and community.

It was only a couple of weeks after the concert that, scrolling through numerous YouTube videos, I discovered that the voice who had called upon people to sing, dance and rejoice was that of former Libyan President Muammar al-Gadhafi. That Hello Psychaleppo had sampled parts of a speech al-Gadhafi had given in July 2011 to a crowd that had assembled on the Green Square in Tripoli to publicly prove their loyalty to the Libyan dictator,

---

[82] https://youtu.be/SOoaGo_drk0?t=2871.

while the country's NATO-backed civil war was ongoing.[83] Besides attesting to the excavational impulse that Hello Psychaleppo's samples may generate among some of his fans, this 'discovery' together with the sense of 'insider knowledge' that it temporarily instilled, highlights an important point when seeking to understand the communities that form around electro-tarab as well as the kind of pleasure it may produce in its listeners. To illustrate this point, we shall, by way of conclusion, return to the memory of the *sammi'ah*, Aleppo's famous connoisseur listeners, and to the image of the yellow man that flashed up at the end of Hello Psychaleppo's 'Shahba' video and which reappeared on the flyer of tonight's concert.

In an interview given to ethnomusicologist Ali Jihad Racy in Santa Monica, California in 1990, Aleppo's legendary singer Sabah Fakhri described his relationship with the sammi'ah in the following way:

As a matter of fact, I feel delighted when I see the people understanding me and judiciously following what I am performing (*bīḥāsbūnī*). Indeed, I prefer an audience that is fully able to fathom my music, one that is learned and artistically enlightened. First and foremost, a listener has to love music because the more he loves it, if he is also able to understand the words and the tunes, the more his presence delights me. Such a listener knows the value of the music, as the jeweller can tell diamond from glass. Of course I sense people's reactions from their movements and by observing their inner emotional tribulations (*infi'āl*) and their responses (*tajāwub*) to what I am singing. (Racy 1991: 8)

The particular nature of intimacy that Fakhri describes as shaping a musical community in the world of tarab has since been defined by authors in numerous ways. Charles Hirschkind (2006: 51) calls it 'the "enchantment" produced by the affective synthesis of listener and performer', whose characteristic 'transsubjective dynamism ... depends on the skills and knowledge of both performer and audience and on the social and technological forms that mediate their relationship'. Michael Frishkopf (2001: 233–4) renders it as the 'relation of harmony (*insijam*)' and the 'exchange of feeling (*tabadul al-shu'ur*)' between performer and listener, as the 'melting (*dhawb*) of the two into one'. Moreover, scholars have associated the ability to *experience* this intimacy with an 'eastern soul', the *ruḥ sharqiyyah,* which Jonathan Shannon (2006: 45) states is a 'key yet elusive element of Arab musical aesthetics' and which Racy (2003: 196) characterises as 'a certain locally based form of cultural-emotional attuning'.

---

[83] Only a few months later, on 20 October 2011, al-Gadhafi was defeated and executed by rebels militants. For a television broadcast that includes the original speech, see https://youtu.be/t51GPvuSiMc.

Steering away from an essentialist reading, these definitions invite one to consider that, in the world of (electro-)tarab, the experience of musical enchantment relies on the recognition not only of the *virtuosity* but also of the *social meaning* of the music one hears.[84] The ideal audience that Hello Psychaleppo envisions for his music, the 'electro-sammiʿah' as we may call them, and which he addresses in the already mentioned title of his first album *Gool L'Ah* ('Say "Ah"' in Arabic), are not only connoisseur listeners of both tarab and electronic dance music, they are also those who are familiar with his samples' old and new cultural, historical and socio-political referents. In other words, they are *deep* listeners, not only in Judith Becker's sense of being deeply touched by music, but also in that by recognising the original musical, lyrical or sonic material, they are able to understand and *be affected* by the samples' new message and function, whether the mobilisation of Abu Arab's poem as a comment on a shared Palestinian-Syrian experience of a lost homeland, or the re-appropriation of meanings generated by political dictatorship by turning the speech of Ghaddafi into a call for musical pleasure in times of displacement.

A definition of what, in the world of (electro)-tarab, constitutes the ideal (electro-) sammiʿah' also has ramifications for our understanding of the social effect of Hello Psychaleppo's samples. This effect can be illustrated via the image of the yellow man, a figure that, as pointed out earlier, has ingrained itself in the urban Aleppian imagination. Just as the identity of the yellow man – the Aleppian resident Abou Zakkour – is only familiar to those who have been to the city or heard stories about him, Hello Psychaleppo's samples can be perceived as 'codes': their recognition has the potential, if only temporarily, to forge a sense of (musical) community and render musical pleasure as an experience of intimacy. It is precisely in this vein that Eldahr has described performing concerts before people who 'recognise' his samples as 'feeling like being home'.[85] Of course, for both Eldahr and his fans (those present tonight or those afar), such 'feelings of home' are made up of different, at times overlapping at times separate, layers of historical, social and cultural intimacy. These range from an affiliation with what social scientist Graham St. John (2003: 65) has called the global and 'neo-tribal-like' 'post-Rave technocultures', an ability to understand Arabic, a lived and/or imagined alignment with the Palestinian struggle, familiarity with sampled songs from previous contexts to a very personal memory of home.

---

[84] An anti-essentialist reading has also informed recent explorations of (post-)tarab as 'affective politics' (Figueroa 2022, Sprengel 2020).

[85] Personal conversation, 16 November 2016.

Back on the dancefloor, Eldahr reminds the audience that for now their 'life in common' has come to an end. 'Every time it gets dark, remember me', the voice proclaims in the concert's official last song. Entitled 'Beirut', this is a farewell song and homage that he wrote before moving to the United States. Then, the audience requests 'Tarab Dub', and with it the voice of Um Kalthoum fills the air: '*wal kun yenawwar bil-'amr* ... [the universe is illuminated by the moon ...]'. Those familiar with the tune sing along in unison: ' ... *ama al-ḥabiiiiiib, al-ḥabiiiiiib, al-ḥabiiiiiib, nur al-'ayun, nur al-'ayun!* [... but the loved one, the loved one is the light of the eyes!]'. When Um Kalthoum, accompanied by the choir that is part of the original sample, sings a *layali*,[86] someone near me cries out: '*Lk Allaaah*!! [O Gooood!]'. 'He is the King of Taste!' one fan praises Hello Psychaleppo after the concert. The person next to him agrees: 'His work is clean. He is classical.'

5 Conclusion

'It may well be', writes ethnomusicologist Timothy Taylor (2001: 139–40) in his book *Strange Sounds – Music Technology and Culture*, 'that one of the reasons that sampling has itself become a kind of art form is that it provides aural glimpses of the social, metonymized into fragments of acoustic musicking, but in their new contexts of electronically generated music, these glimpses are historical.' Taylor has placed the social and historical significance of sampling into a context where technological possibilities have turned music-making into an increasingly individualised and isolated activity. Hello Psychaleppo and the many other Syrian electronic musicians mentioned in this Element, too, produce their music from a position of isolation. This position, however is as much compelled by forced migration than it is generated by digital technology. Within this context, samples relate to the past, by paying homage to left behind places and musical ancestors, the present, by forging a transnational musical community, and the future, by paving the way for new (electronic) forms of (Arab) music.

Electro-tarab is predominantly consumed by a young, urban and largely middle-class audience. To more conservative tarab consumers (such as those who exclusively associate tarab with high-art, pre-First World War traditions or who historically rationalise it in opposition to Western music), it may trigger anxieties about the technological 'corruption' of established musical norms and notions of musical purity not unlike those provoked when the term tarab was applied to the mass-mediated music of Egyptian mega-stars such as Abd al-Halim Hafiz (Stokes 2009). This Element has avoided taking Hello

---

[86] As mentioned earlier, a layali is a vocal improvisation on the syllable 'ya layl [O night]' that is characteristic of traditional vocal tarab.

Psychaleppo's claim to the word tarab as an occasion to 'test' his musical practice against the different notions of authenticity that characterise existing discourses (although it has outlined how this claim is rooted in a memory of Aleppo's musical legacy). Rather, I have aimed to shift the focus towards an investigation of the socio-political spaces and imaginaries of home that are associated with his practice of sampling. From nostalgic paths of return to an Aleppo of the past, the pleasure of dancing to acoustic fragments of a shared Palestinian-Syrian history, the 'revolution' that one fan heard in Psychaleppo's music, to the joint mobilisation of a universe 'illuminated by the moon' at a time when much of the region has been overwhelmed by 'the gloom' of a dictatorial backlash that political theorist Gilbert Achcar (2016: 17) has described as 'an "Arab Winter"' – my intention has been to highlight that Hello Psychaleppo's stated goal of 'bringing back to life tarab' describes more than the desire to give this music a new identity. Rather, it evokes a claim to the musical memory of a city that, due to the workings of war, an authoritarian regime and global media outlets that have tended to exclusively render Aleppo as an 'icon of destruction', has become largely imperceptible. It credits music (particularly samples) with the power, even temporarily, to collapse the distance that separates people, places and communities and create new forms of belonging. And it offers a way to complexify our understanding of musical meaning making, creativity and experimentation during Syria's devastating years of war and the ongoing history of displacement that it has generated.

6 Epilogue: Diasporas of Hope

A year after Hello Psychaleppo's concert in Beirut, I received a parcel from his new home in the United States containing the hand-made CD case of his 2017 album *TOYOUR* (Arabic for 'birds'). Looking at the front album cover, I see a group of human-like creatures gazing up at the sky with their mouths open (Figure 8). They look astonished, as if they have spotted something in the far distance. As I open the case, I find not only the CD but also a shimmering hologram sticker of a feather. Similar to the yellow man from the 'Shahba' video, I soon understand this feather to be a code. Its background story goes something like this: 'It was in China, late one moonless night/the Simurgh first appeared to mortal sight/he let a feather float down through the air/and rumours of its fame spread everywhere/throughout the world men separately conceived/an image of its shape, and all believed/their private fantasies uniquely true!' (Attar 2011: 44).

These verses are from *The Conference of the Birds*, a work of poetry by Farid al-Din Attar (ca. 1145–1221), one of the pivotal figures of the Iranian Sufi poetic tradition. Conceived as an allegory for the mystical quest for divine

Figure 8 Cover art for *TOYOUR* Courtesy of Samer Saem Eldahr

truth and unity in god, *The Conference of the Birds* depicts the journey of thirty birds. In their search for the legendary *Simurgh* bird that is said to reside beyond the mystical mountain *Qaf* and guided by the hoopoe bird, who resembles the role of an Islamic Sheikh, they travel through seven valleys – the spiritual 'stations' (*maqamat*) of the Sufi path – only to finally discover that they themselves are the Simurgh (Pers. *si morgh* = thirty birds) (see Safi 2007; Stone 2006: 95).

Inspired by Attar's poetry, Hello Psychaleppo spent over three years compiling a digital archive of hundreds of Arab songs that reference birds or evoke the theme of flying, ten of which he eventually sampled on the album. The result not only takes his own transformation into a bird that marked the end of the 'Shahba' video onto a different, musical level; it also transposes *The Conference of the Birds* to contemporary Syrian history. As he explained, to him the Simurgh embodies both the concept of divine unity and summons up a 'poetic scenery of maybe what Syrians collectively think' or 'where we're heading towards'.[87] Or, as he explained elsewhere: 'Birds really do have freedom in its natural sense. They can fly everywhere, they can be loud everywhere. To have that perspective on life is huge, and something that we as Syrians, or Palestinians, or Egyptians – there's a similarity in our stories. It's no longer just displaced Palestinians. But there's a longing for that freedom, even if it's something you've never really had to that extent.'[88]

---

[87] www.alaraby.co.uk/english/society/2017/3/17/hello-psychaleppo-the-world-is-pretty-surreal-right-now.

[88] www.albawaba.com/entertainment/hello-psychaleppo-interview-syrian-music-party-dj-arabic-music-1019218.

'*Ya tuyur*! [O Birds!]', is how the famous Syrian-Egyptian singer Asmahan addresses her listeners in the album's opening track, followed by a message that is underlined by the majestic sounds of the original sample's Middle Eastern string orchestra: 'Sing of my love, chant my passion and hopes! Sing of my love, chant my passion and hopes! [*Ghanni ḥubbi wa anshudi wagdi wa amali. Ghanni ḥubbi wa anshudi wagdi wa amali!*].[89] This final glimpse into the work of Hello Psychaleppo may help us understand that the feather hidden in *TOYOUR*'s CD case is meant to forge what the scholar Arjun Appadurai has described as 'diasporas of hope' (Appadurai 1996: 6). Or, as one of Hello Psychaleppo's fans has commented on SoundCloud: 'Memories of the past blend with hopes for the future.'[90]

---

[89] For a recording of the album's opening track, see www.youtube.com/watch?v=O-6SQjdgdg4. For the original sample, see www.youtube.com/watch?v=2p80t6vJUL8. Born in Syria in 1912, Asmahan spent most of her life in Egypt where she died in a mysterious car accident in 1944. The melody of '*Ya tuyur*' was composed by Egyptian composer Muhammad al-Qasabji in 1940. The song is said to have initially been intended for her rival Um Kalthoum but was given to Asmahan since her voice was more suited and able to carry out the song's 'Queen of the night' section (Zuhur 2000: 101).

[90] https://soundcloud.com/hellopsychaleppo/tarab-dub.

References

Achcar, G. (2016). *Morbid Symptoms: Relapse in the Arab Uprising*. London: Saqi Books.

——— (2013). *The People Want: A Radical Exploration of the Arab Uprising*. London: Saqi Books.

Alaghband-Zadeh, C. (2017). Listening to North Indian Classical Music: How Embodied Ways of Listening Perform Imagined Histories and Social Class. *Ethnomusicology* 61 (2), 207–33.

Anon. (2015). *Death of Aleppo*. Documentary. Al Jazeera World.

Appadurai, A. (1996). *Modernity at Large: Cultural Dimensions of Globalization*. Minneapolis: University of Minnesota Press.

Armbrust, W. (2001). The Impact of the Media on Egyptian Music. In Danielson, V., Marcus, S. & Reynolds, D. (eds.), *Garland Encyclopedia of World Music*, vol. 6, *The Middle East*. London: Routledge, pp. 232–242.

Attar, F. a.D. (2011). *The Conference of the Birds*. Translated by Darbandi, A. & Davis, D. London: Penguin Books.

Azaryahu, M. (2007). *Tel Aviv: Mythography of a City*. Syracuse: Syracuse University Press.

Baily, J. & Collyer, M. (2006). Introduction: Music and Migration. *Journal of Ethnic and Migration Studies* 32 (2), 167–82.

Barakeh, K. (2014). Regarding the Pain of Others and Damascus. In Halasa, M., Omareen, Z. & Mahfoud, N. (eds.), *Syria Speaks Art and Culture from the Frontline*. London: Saqi, pp. 157–64.

Barthes, R. (2013 [1957]). *Mythologies*. Translated by Howard, R. New York: Hill and Wang.

Bascom, W. (1965). The Forms of Folklore: Prose Narratives. *The Journal of American Folklore* 78 (307), 3–20.

Becker, J. (2004). *Deep Listeners: Music, Emotion, and Trancing*. Bloomington: Indiana University Press.

Behdad, A. (1994). *Belated Travelers: Orientalism in the Age of Colonial Dissolution*. Cork: Cork University Press.

Born, G. (2013). *Music, Sound and Space: Transformations of Public and Private Experience*. Cambridge: Cambridge University Press.

Burkhalter, T. (2013). *Local Music Scenes and Globalization: Transnational Platforms in Beirut*. New York: Routledge.

Burkhalter, T., Dickinson, K. & Harbert, B. (2013). *The Arab Avant-Garde: Music, Politics, Modernity*. Middletown: Wesleyan University Press.

Cabot, H. (2016). 'Refugee Voices': Tragedy, Ghosts, and the Anthropology of Not Knowing. *Journal of Contemporary Ethnography* 45 (6), 645–72.

Chatty, D. (2017). *Syria: The Making and Unmaking of a Refuge State*. London: Hurst & Co.

(2014). Anthropology and Forced Migration. In Fiddian-Qasmiyeh, E., Loescher, G., Long, K. & Sigona, N. (eds.), *The Oxford Handbook of Refugee and Forced Migration Studies*. Oxford: Oxford University Press, pp. 74–85.

Dalal, M. Q. (2006a). *al-Qudud al-diniyah: baḥth tarikhi wa-musiqi fi al-qudud al-Ḥalabiyah* [The Religious Qudud: A Historical and Musical Study of the Aleppian Qudud]. Damascus: Wizarat al-Thaqafah fi al-Jumhuriyah al-'Arabiyah al-Suriyah.

(2006b). *Shaykh al-mutribin Sabri Mudallal wa-athar Ḥalab fi ghina'ihi wa-alḥanih: dirasah taḥliliyah musiqiyah li-turath Ḥalab al-ghina'i* [Shaykh al-mutribin – Sabri Mudallal and the Influence of Aleppo in His Song and Compositions: A Musical and Analytical Study of the Vocal Heritage of Aleppo]. Damascus: Wizarat al-Thaqafah fi al-Jumhuriyah al-'Arabiyah al-Suriyah.

Danielson, V. (1997). *The Voice of Egypt: Umm Kulthum, Arabic Song, and Egyptian Society in the Twentieth Century*. Chicago: University of Chicago Press.

Demerdash, N. (2012). Consuming Revolution: Ethics, Art, and Ambivalence in the Arab Spring. *New Middle Eastern Studies* 2, 1–17.

Fabian, J. (1983). *Time and the Other: How Anthropology Makes Its Object*. New York: Columbia University Press.

Farmer, H. G. (1930). *Historical Facts for the Arabian Musical Influence*. London: William Reeves.

Figueroa, M. A. (2022). Post-Tarab: Music and Affective Politics in the US SWANA Diaspora. *Ethnomusicology* 66 (2), 236–263.

Frishkopf, M. (2021). Musical Journeys. In Bayat, A. & Herrera, L. (eds.), *Global Middle East: Into the Twenty-First Century*. Berkeley: University of California Press, pp. 157–74.

(ed.). (2010). *Music and Media in the Arab World*. Cairo: American University in Cairo Press.

(2001). Tarab in the Mystic Sufi Chant of Egypt. In Zuhur, S. (ed.), *Colors of Enchantment: Theater, Dance, Music, and the Visual Arts of the Middle East*. Cairo: American University in Cairo Press, pp. 239–76.

Fulton-Melanson, J. (2022). Post-Tarab Identities in Diaspora: A Sonic Imaginary of Arab Canada. In Abdelhady, D. & Aly, R. (eds.), *Routledge Handbook on Middle Eastern Diasporas*. London: Routledge, pp. 197–208.

Fulton-Melanson, J. (2021). The Post-Tarab Soundscape: Underground Electronic Dance Music Culture and the Arab-Canadian Diaspora. Unpublished PhD dissertation, York University.

Gabiam, N. (2016). *The Politics of Suffering: Syria's Palestinian Refugee Camps*. Bloomington: Indiana University Press.

Gill, D. (2017). *Melancholic Modalities: Affect, Islam, and Turkish Classical Musicians*. New York: Oxford University Press.

Glasser, J. (2016). *The Lost Paradise: Andalusi Music in Urban North Africa*. Chicago: University of Chicago Press.

Goodwin, A. (1988). Sample and Hold: Pop Music in the Digital Age of Reproduction, *Critical Quarterly* 30 (3), 34–49.

Habash, D. (2021). 'Do Like You Did in Aleppo': Negotiating Space and Place among Syrian Musicians in Istanbul. *Journal of Refugee Studies* 34 (2), 1370–86.

Hajj, H. (2016). The Syrian Musicians in Istanbul: The Relationship between Repertoire and Stage. *Alternatif Politika* 8, 474–84.

al-Haj Saleh, Y. (2017). *Impossible Revolution: Making Sense of the Syrian Tragedy*. London: Hurst Publishers.

Halasa, M., Omareen, Z. & Mahfoud N. (eds.) (2014). *Syria Speaks: Art and Culture from the Frontline*. London: Saqi Books.

al-Hardan, A. (2016). *Palestinians in Syria: Nakba Memories of Shattered Communities*. New York: Columbia University Press.

Hawas, S. (2012). Global Translations and Translating the Global: Discursive Regimes of Revolt. In Mehrez, S. (ed.), *Translating Egypt's Revolution: The Language of Tahrir*. New York: Cairo University Press, pp. 277–305.

Hirschkind, C. (2006). *The Ethical Soundscape: Cassette Sermons and Islamic Counterpublics*. New York: Columbia University Press.

Hirshberg, J. (1990). Radical Displacement, Post Migration Conditions and Traditional Music. *The World of Music* 32 (3), 68–89.

Iino, L. (2009). Inheriting the Ghammāz-Oriented Tradition: D'Erlanger and Aleppine Maqām Practice Observed. *Ethnomusicology Forum* 18 (2), 261–80.

Ismail, S. (2011). The Syrian Uprising: Imagining and Performing the Nation. *Studies in Ethnicity and Nationalism* 11, 538–49.

Jarjour, T. (2018). *Sense and Sadness: Syriac Chant in Aleppo*. New York: Oxford University Press.

Jasim, A. (2016). The Development of New Political Subjectivities amongst Syria's Palestinians during the Syrian Uprising. Unpublished MA thesis, Philipps University of Marburg.

Karkabi, N. (2020). Self-Liberated Citizens: Unproductive Pleasures, Loss of Self, and Playful Subjectivities in Palestinian Raves. *Anthropological Quarterly* 93 (4), 679–708.

(2018). Electro-Dabke: Performing Cosmopolitan Nationalism and Borderless Humanity. *Public Culture* 30 (1), 173–96.

Katz, I. J. (2015). *Henry George Farmer and the First International Congress of Arab Music (Cairo 1932)*. Leiden: Brill.

Khalili, L. (2007). *Heroes and Martyrs of Palestine: The Politics of National Commemoration*. Cambridge: Cambridge University Press.

al-Khateeb, A., Rollins, T. & Shaheen, A. (2020). *A New Palestinian Community? Syria's Uprising and Conflict, from the Perspective of the Palestinian Camps*. Berlin: Rosa Luxemburg Stiftung. www.rosalux.de/en/publication/id/42803/a-new-palestinian-community.

Kligman, M. L. (2009). *Maqam and Liturgy: Ritual, Music, and Aesthetics of Syrian Jews in Brooklyn*. Detroit: Wayne State University Press.

Lacroix, T. & Fiddian-Qasmiyeh, E. (2013.) Refugee and Diaspora Memories: The Politics of Remembering and Forgetting. *Journal of Intercultural Studies* 34 (6), 684–96.

Levi, E. & Scheding, F. (2010). *Music and Displacement: Diasporas, Mobilities, and Dislocations in Europe and Beyond*. Lanham: Scarecrow Press.

Lidskog, R. (2016). The Role of Music in Ethnic Identity Formation in Diaspora: A Research Review. *International Social Science Journal* 66, 23–38.

Lohman, L. (2010). *Umm Kulthūm: Artistic Agency and the Shaping of an Arab Legend, 1967–2007*. Middletown: Wesleyan University Press.

Lenssen, A. (2020). The Filmmaker as Artisan: An Interview with the Members of Abounaddara. *Third Text* 34 (1), 159–71.

Manuel, P. (1995). Music as Symbol, Music as Simulacrum: Postmodern, Pre-Modern, and Modern Aesthetics in Subcultural Popular Musics. *Popular Music* 14 (2), 227–39.

Martin, S. (ed.) (2008). *Recycling Culture(s)*. Newcastle: Cambridge Scholars.

Massad, J. (2003). Liberating Songs: Palestine Put to Music. *Journal of Palestine Studies*, 32 (3), 21–38.

McLeod, K. & DiCola, P. (2011). *Creative License: The Law and Culture of Digital Sampling*. Durham: Duke University Press.

McDonald, D. A. (2013). *My Voice Is My Weapon*. Durham: Duke University Press.

Miller, P. D. (ed.) (2008). *Sound Unbound: Sampling Digital Music and Culture*. Cambridge, MA: MIT Press.

Morris, B. (2008). 1948: *A History of the First Arab-Israeli War.* New Haven: Yale University Press.

Munif, Y. (2020). *The Syrian Revolution: Between the Politics of Life and the Geopolitics of Death.* London: Pluto Press.

Navas, E. (2012). *Remix Theory the Aesthetics of Sampling.* Vienna: Springer Verlag.

Nelson, K. (1985). *The Art of Reciting the Qur'an.* Austin: University of Texas Press

Nickell, C. (2020) Promises and Pitfalls: The Two-Faced Nature of Streaming and Social Media Platforms for Beirut-Based Independent Musicians. *Popular Communication* 18 (1), 48–64.

Nooshin, L. (2018), 'Our Angel of Salvation': Towards an Understanding of Iranian Cyberspace as an Alternative Sphere of Musical Sociality. *Ethnomusicology*, 62 (3), 341–74.

Öğüt, E. H. (2021). Music, Migration, and Public Space: Syrian Street Music in the Political Context. *Arts* 10 (4), article 71.

Ong, W. (1982). *Orality and Literacy: The Technologizing of the Word.* London: Methuen.

Parker, J. D. (2018). Song and Rebellion in the Syrian Uprising. *Middle Eastern Studies*, 54 (6): 1015–28.

Pearlman, W. (2017). *We Crossed a Bridge and It Trembled: Voices from Syria.* New York: Custom House.

Pinto, P. G. (2016). Mystical Bodies/Unruly Bodies: Experience, Empowerment and Subjectification in Syrian Sufism. *Social Compass*, 63 (2), 197–212.

(2006). Sufism, Moral Performance and the Public Sphere in Syria. *Revue des Mondes Musulmans et de la Méditerranée* 115–16, 155–171.

Poché, C. (2001). Musical Life in Aleppo. In Danielson, V., Marcus, S. & Reynolds, D. (eds.), *Garland Encyclopedia of World Music,* vol. 6, *The Middle East.* London: Routledge, pp. 594–600.

Racy, A. J. (2003). *Making Music in the Arab World.* Cambridge: Cambridge University Press.

(1991). Creativity and Ambience: An Ecstatic Feedback Model from Arab Music. *The World of Music* 33 (3), 7–28.

Raja'i, F. & Darwish, N.A. (1955). *Min kunuzina: al-Muwashshaḥat al-Andalusiyyah* [From Our Heritage: The Andalusian Muwashshaḥat]. Aleppo: Maṭbaʿat al-Sharq.

Ramsay, G. & Askland, H. H. (2022). Displacement as Condition: A Refugee, a Farmer and the Teleology of Life, *Ethnos* 87 (3), 600–21.

Rasmussen, A. K. (1996). Theory and Practice at the 'Arabic Org': Digital Technology in Contemporary Arab Music Performance. *Popular Music* 15 (3), 345–65.

Rasmussen, A. K., Impey, A., Willson, R. B. & Aksoy. O. (2019). Call and Response: SEM President's Roundtable 2016, 'Ethnomusicological Responses to the Contemporary Dynamics of Migrants and Refugees'. *Ethnomusicology* 63 (2), 279–314.

Reyes, A. (1999). *Songs of the Caged, Songs of the Free: Music and the Vietnamese Refugee Experience*. Philadelphia: Temple University Press.

Rietveld, H. (2011). Infinite Noise Spirals: The Musical Cosmopolitanism of Psytrance. In St. John, G. (ed.), *The Local Scenes and Global Culture of Psytrance*. London: Routledge, pp. 69–88.

Rodgers, T. (2003). On the Process and Aesthetics of Sampling in Electronic Music Production. *Organised Sound* 8 (3), 313–20.

Rose, T. (1994). *Black Noise: Rap Music and Black Culture in Contemporary America*. Middletown: Wesleyan University Press.

Sa'di, A. H. & Abu-Lughod, L. (eds.) (2007). *Nakba: Palestine, 1948, and the Claims of Memory*. New York: Columbia University Press.

Safi, O. (2007). 'Aṭṭar, Farid Al-Din. In Fleet, K., Krämer, G., Matringe, D., Nawas, J., and Rowson, K. (eds.), *Encyclopaedia of Islam*. Leiden: Brill Reference Online. http://dx.doi.org/10.1163/1573-3912_ei3_COM_23976.

Shannon, J. H. (2019). From Silence into Song: Affective Horizons and Nostalgic Dwelling among Syrian Musicians in Istanbul. *Rast Musicology Journal* 7 (2), 2050–64.

　(2018). Nightingales and Sweet Basil: The Cultural Geography of Aleppine Song. In Frishkopf, M. & Spinetti, F. (eds.), *Music, Sound, and Architecture in Islam*. Austin: University of Texas Press, pp. 146–65.

　(2016). Sounding Home: Syrian Musicians in Istanbul. *Anthropology News* 57 (5–6), 8–9.

　(2006). *Among the Jasmine Trees: Music and Modernity in Contemporary Syria*. Middletown: Wesleyan University Press.

　(2003a). al-Muwashshahât and al-Qudûd al-Halabiyya: Two Genres in the Aleppine Wasla. *Middle East Studies Association Bulletin* 37 (1), 82–101.

　(2003b). Sultans of Spin: Syrian Sacred Music on the World Stage. *American Anthropologist* 105 (2), 266–77.

　(2003c). Emotion, Performance, and Temporality in Arab Music: Reflections on Tarab. *Cultural Anthropology* 18 (1), 72–98.

Shelemay, K. K. (1998). *Let Jasmine Rain Down: Song and Remembrance Among Syrian Jews*. Chicago: University of Chicago Press.

Sigona, N. (2014). The Politics of Refugee Voices: Representations, Narratives, and Memories. In Fiddian-Qasmiyeh, E., Loescher, G., Long, K. & Sigona, N. (eds.), *The Oxford Handbook of Refugee and Forced Migration Studies*. Oxford: Oxford University Press, pp. 369–82.

Silverstein, S. (2016). The Punk Arab: Demystifying Omar Souleyman's Techno-Dabke. In Veal, M. E. & Tammy, K. E. (eds.), *Punk Ethnography: Artists and Scholars Listen to Sublime Frequencies*. Middletown: Wesleyan University Press, pp. 265–87.

(2012). Syria's Radical Dabka. *Middle East Report* 263. https://merip.org/2012/05/syrias-radical-dabka/.

De Sousa Santos, B. (2018). *The End of the Cognitive Empire: The Coming of Age of Epistemologies of the South*. Durham: Duke University Press.

Sprengel, D. (2020). Street Concerts and Sexual Harassment in Post-Mubarak Egypt: Ṭarab as Affective Politics. In Fischlin, D. & Porter, E. (eds.), *Playing for Keeps: Improvisation in the Aftermath*, New York: Duke University Press, pp. 160–90.

St John, G. (2013). Aliens Are Us: Cosmic Liminality, Remixticism, and Alienation in Psytrance. *The Journal of Religion and Popular Culture* 25 (2), 186–204.

(2003). Post-Rave Technotribalism and the Carnival of Protest. In Muggleton, D. & Weinzierl, R. (eds.), *The Post-Subcultures Reader*. Oxford: Berg, pp. 65–82.

Stokes, M. (2020). Migration and Music. *Music Research Annual* 1, 1–24.

(2009). 'Abd al-Halim's Microphone. In Nooshin, L. (ed.), *Music and the Play of Power in the Middle East, North Africa and Central Asia*. Farnham: Ashgate Press, pp. 55–73.

Stone, C. (2008). Fayruz, the Rahbani Brothers, Jerusalem, and the Leba-stinian Song. In Mayer, T., & Mourad, S. A. (eds.), *Jerusalem: Idea and Reality*. London: Routledge, pp. 155–67.

(2007). *Popular Culture and Nationalism in Lebanon: The Fairouz and Rahbani Nation*. London: Routledge.

Stone, L. (2006). Blessed Perplexity: The Topos of Ḥayrat in ʿAṭṭār's Manṭiq al-Ṭayr. In Lewisohn, L. & Shackle, C. (eds.), *ʿAttar and the Persian Sufi Tradition: The Art of Spiritual Flight*. London: Tauris Publishers, pp. 95–111.

Swedenburg, T. (1990) The Palestinian Peasant as National Signifier. *Anthropological Quarterly* 63 (1), 18–30.

Tahhan, S. (2008). *Al-ḥakawati al-suri* [The Syrian Storyteller]. Damascus: Dār Kanʿān.

Tahhan, S. & Rugh, A. B. (2005). *Folktales from Syria*. Austin: University of Texas Press.

Taylor, T. D. (2016). Neoliberal Capitalism and the Rise of Digital Sampling. In Bull, M. & Back, L., (eds.), *The Auditory Culture Reader* (2nd ed.). London: Routledge, pp. 445–52.

⸺ (2001). *Strange Sounds: Music, Technology and Culture*. London: Routledge.

Touma, H. H. (1996). *The Music of the Arabs*. Portland: Amadeus Press.

Wedeen, L. (2019). *Authoritarian Apprehensions Ideology, Judgment, and Mourning in Syria*. Chicago: University of Chicago Press.

Wenz, C. (in press). 'I Say She Is a Muṭriba': Memories of Aleppo's Jewish Female Musicians. In Fruehauf, T. (ed.), *The Oxford Handbook of Jewish Music*. New York: Oxford University Press.

Wiedemann, F. 2019. Remixing Battle Rap and Arabic Poetic Battling. *Rivista sul Mediterraneo islamico / Università della Calabria* 4, 13–28.

Yassin-Kassab, R. & Al-Shami, L. (2016). *Burning Country: Syrians in Revolution and War*. London: Pluto Press.

Zuhur, S. (2000). *Asmahan's Secrets: Woman, War and Song*. Austin: University of Texas Press.

This Element draws on several years of multi-sited fieldwork carried out in Berlin, Beirut, Tel Aviv and Istanbul. Most of this fieldwork was undertaken in the context of my PhD research (2015–19), which was funded by a doctoral studentship of the German National Academic Foundation and the Mildred Loss Studentship of the Jewish Music Institute (JMI) in London. I would like to thank Ilana Webster-Kogen, Edwin Seroussi, Muzna Awayed-Bishara, Ahmed al-Khashem and Ansar Jasim for their valuable feedback and comments; Yosef Antebi, Lamis Sirees, Abdallah Rahhal, Ahmed Basaleh (Abu Farraj), Hanna M. Issa, Nihad Alabsi, Philippe Zarif, Mohammed Dibo, Omar Kaddour, Al-Hakam Shaar and Muhammad Najjar for kindly sharing with me their insights into Aleppo's past and present (musical) lives; and Omar Shammah, Sedki Alimam and Bashar Salloum for giving me the permission to include their artwork. I am especially grateful to Samer Saem Eldahr (Hello Psychaleppo) for introducing me to the world of electro-tarab. His musical creativity has been the main inspiration for my writing. Many thanks are also due to the editors of this series, Laudan Nooshin and Simon McVeigh as well as the editorial staff at Cambridge University Press. Their guidance and critical reading have greatly improved this work.

Cambridge Elements ☰

Music and the City

Simon McVeigh

Goldsmiths, University of London

Simon McVeigh is Professor of Music at Goldsmiths, University of London, and President of the Royal Musical Association. His research focuses on British musical life 1700–1945; and on violin music and performance practices of the period. Books include *Concert Life in London from Mozart to Haydn* (Cambridge) and *The Italian Solo Concerto 1700– 1760* (Boydell). Current work centres on London concert life around 1900: a substantial article on the London Symphony Orchestra was published in 2013 and a book exploring London's musical life in the Edwardian era is in preparation for Boydell. He is also co-investigator on the digital concert-programme initiative *InConcert*.

Laudan Nooshin

City, University of London

Laudan Nooshin is Professor in Music at City University, London. She has research interests in creative processes in Iranian music; music and youth culture in Iran; urban sound; music in Iranian cinema and music and gender. Her publications include *Iranian Classical Music: The Discourses and Practice of Creativity* (2015, Ashgate, awarded the 2016 British Forum for Ethnomusicology Book Prize); *Music and the Play of Power in the Middle East, North Africa and Central Asia* (ed. 2009, Ashgate) and *The Ethnomusicology of Western Art Music* (ed. 2013, Routledge), as well as numerous journal articles and book chapters. Between 2007 and 2011, Laudan was co-editor of the journal *Ethnomusicology Forum*.

About the Series

Elements in Music and the City sets urban musical cultures within new global and cross-disciplinary perspectives
The series aims to open up new ways of thinking about music in an urban context, embracing the widest diversity of music and sound in cities across the world. Breaking down boundaries between historical and contemporary, and between popular and high art, it seeks to illuminate the diverse urban environment in all its exhilarating and vivid complexity. The urban thus becomes a microcosm of a much messier, yet ultimately much richer, conception of the 'music of everyday life'.
Rigorously peer-reviewed and written by leading scholars in their fields, each Element offers authoritative and challenging approaches towards a fast-developing area of music research. Elements in Music and the City will present extended case-studies within a comparative perspective, while developing pioneering new theoretical frameworks for an emerging field.
The series is inherently cross-disciplinary and global in its perspective, as reflected in the wide-ranging multi-national advisory board. It will encourage a similar diversity of approaches, ranging from the historical and ethnomusicological to contemporary popular music and sound studies.
Written in a clear, engaging style without the need for specialist musical knowledge, *Elements in Music and the City* aims to fill the demand for easily accessible, quality texts available for teaching and research. It will be of interest not only to researchers and students in music and related arts, but also to a broad range of readers intrigued by how we might understand music and sound in its social, cultural and political contexts

Cambridge Elements $\equiv$

Music and the City

Elements in the Series

Popular Music Heritage, Cultural Justice and the Deindustrialising City
Sarah Baker, Zelmarie Cantillon and Raphaël Nowak

Music from Aleppo during the Syrian War
Clara Wenz

A full series listing is available at: www.cambridge.org/emtc

Printed in the United States
by Baker & Taylor Publisher Services